The Psalms of Children:
Their Songs and Laments

Understanding & Healing
the Scars on the Souls
of Children

The Psalms of Children: Their Songs and Laments

Understanding & Healing the Scars on the Souls of Children

Ursula M. Anderson,
M.B.Ch.B., M.R.C.S., D.P.H., D.C.H., F.A.A.P.,
D.Sc. Hon.

with **James T. Doyle,** M.Div.

Foreword by
His Holiness The Dalai Lama

She-Bear Publications
Ellicottville, New York

Published by

SHE-BEAR PUBLICATIONS

FIRST EDITION

ISBN (HardCover): 0-9655435-1-X
ISBN (SoftCover): 0-9655435-0-1

Book Design: James T. Doyle
Illustrations: Robin Clark

Dedication

To the Memories that arrived with me
on Planet Earth.

To the Memories that the living of my life
rendered to me.

To those souls whose energies collided
with mine to make my journey bumpy,
and to those whose souls encountering mine
made the road smooth.

But above all,
to the children who
in the smooth and bumpy times
taught me that Love and Hope,
and belief in their existence,
is a ceaseless call and a
never ending unfolding of the
Consciousness of Life Divine.

I give my loving gratitude.

About The Title

In their times, the Psalmists of the scriptures were the chronicleers of Life and the purveyors of advice on how to live it. It is my belief that children are the present day Psalmists and, through their words, behaviors, and dilemmas, are telling the world how to restore order and diminish the violence that is tearing it apart.

About The Children

The names of the children from my practice whose stories have been told have been changed to safeguard their identities. Likewise, details from their stories have been omitted to further protect them. It is emphasized that the stories used reflect the stories of countless other children whom I have seen in my practice over the course of many years.

Illustration for Chapter VII

The illustration for Chapter VII was drawn by Joseph, aged 4, who was abandoned by his drug addicted mother and now lives with his grandparents. He shows himself standing apart from his mother whom he rarely sees and his two younger sisters. When asked why, he replied it was because "I feel like Mommy." Clearly this child is feeling in his soul grief at separation from his mother as well as her grief at her separation from the source of all love. It is an eloquent message of the deep sense of loss and disconnectedness children feel when neglected or abandoned by their biological parents even though they are lovingly cared for by grandparents.

Illustration for Chapter VIII

The illustration for Chapter VIII was drawn by Mary, aged 3, the sister of Joseph who drew the illustration for Chapter VII. Asked to draw her family, she totally omitted her mother, placed herself close to her brother and separated them as a pair from their younger sister, Martha, whom she drew to resemble a spider. Clearly she considers Martha an interloper on the bond she feels with Joseph. While Mary and her siblings have loving grandparents, their absence from these "family" portraits tell of how children, even at this young age, perceive family as Mommy, Daddy and children. When biological parents are absent no one can take their place.

Acknowledgments

In these times we are too often led to believe that people do not care about others and that assistance of any kind is brokered at a price. *The Psalms of Children: Their Songs and Laments* has from its conception on February 11, 1996 to its birth on December 8, 1996 proved the contrary to be true and that within every human being there is that which longs to reach and help another.

Several individuals took time from their busy schedules to read the manuscript and render not only their evaluations, but their loving support for the messages of the book; among many in this regard I especially thank Dr. Richard Cox, Dr. John Allan Loftus, and Dr. Norman Shealy.

A special thanks goes to Mrs. Robin Clark who, while enduring the dying and death of her beloved husband, Tom, nevertheless found time to take my ideas and make of them exquisite illustrations. These I dedicate to Tom Clark's memory and to the promise of a full life for Morgan, the four–year–old son of Robin and Tom.

Above all, I recognize with love and appreciation beyond the telling, Mr. James Doyle. I prefer to hand-write rather than use machines. Thus, James took all my hand-written material and its several adjustments and, with unending patience, created the final typed manuscript which went to the printer. Because of his presence, his loving and dedicated support, and the giving of his many gifts, I am perhaps creating precedent by adding his name to mine, not as co-author but as co-producer. The children and I thank you, James.

Finally, I extend my deep gratitude to His Holiness The Dalai Lama for the precious honor he bestowed on the messages of this book and its author by writing a beautiful and compelling Foreword which calls humankind to a re-thinking of its present tenets of whom we are and how we came to be -- which is, indeed, the message of the book.

To all, Within all, and Through all, may the oneness of
The God of All be praised and made manifest.

December 8, 1996

Late have I loved you, O Beauty,
so ancient and so new,
late have I loved you!
And behold, you were within me and
I was outside,
and there I sought for you, and in
my deformity I rushed headlong
into the well-formed things that you
have made.
You were with me, and I was not
with you.
Those outer beauties held me far
from you,
yet if they had not been in you,
they would not have existed at all.
You called, and cried out to me and
broke open my deafness;
you shone forth upon me and you
scattered my blindness:
You breathed fragrance, and I drew
in my breath
and I now pant for you:
I tasted and I hunger and thirst;
you touched me,
and I burned for your peace.

The Confessions of
St. Augustine of Hippo

Contents

Foreword

Nowadays, many children grow up in unhappy homes. If they do not receive proper affection when they are young, in later life they will rarely love their parents and often will find it hard to love others. This is very sad. Since a child cannot survive without the care of others, love is its most important nourishment. The happiness of childhood, the allaying of the child's many fears and the healthy development of its self-confidence all depend directly upon love.

We are completely dependent upon our mother's care from the earliest stages of our growth. Some scientists claim that a pregnant woman's mental state, be it calm or agitated, has a direct effect on her unborn child. Certainly there is a critical period of brain development from the time of birth up to at least the age of three or four, during which time loving physical contact is the single most important factor for the normal growth of the child. If the child is not held, hugged, cuddled or loved, its development will be impaired and its brain will not mature properly.

The accounts of children's sufferings that the author has collected here serve as a caution to us all. I believe that love, kindness and generosity are natural human qualities, but we have to share them unconditionally with all our human brothers and sisters. We are all interdependent and once love and human affection are denied to one person, he or she will deny them to others. These stories are examples of what can happen as a result. I trust that many readers of this book will be moved to realise the importance of love and affection not only in personal relationships, but also in society at large. One way of putting this into effect is to take every opportunity to help those who are unable, like children, to help themselves.

His Holiness The Dalai Lama
November 12, 1996

Prologue

If today you hear his voice,
harden not your hearts.

Psalm 95:8

My aching heart had
turned to stone.

Aidan
A 28–year–old man

If you, O Lord, mark iniquities,
who could stand it?
But with you is forgiveness and kindness
and plenteous redemption.

Psalms 130:3, 7b.

Several years ago I was deeply moved by the words of a 28–year–old man whose death was imminent. He was a prisoner on death row, awaiting execution for the murder of an elderly, defenseless couple whom he didn't know and had never met prior to their deadly encounter. The couple had returned to their home after spending the evening with their children and found him burglarizing it. Confronting him in their living room, he turned and, without a moments hesitation, shot them, then fled with his loot, which was their treasured belongings. At the time this occurred, he was 20 years of age.

Eventually caught and convicted of their murder, he spent several years pursuing many avenues of appeal against his death sentence. When all proved fruitless, he faced his punishment with the equanimity of one who had at last found his way of connecting to the source of his life. This source, which goes by many names and titles, is subsumed, perhaps, in one word - God. During his prison years he spoke eloquently about the felt absence of God during his childhood.

Growing up fatherless and with a well-intentioned mother, herself similarly deprived, he ran the streets to find his connection to life. This he did in abundance with others of similar background. Starting on a life of crime at the age of nine, he skipped school, became a dropout and supported himself handsomely with money earned the dangerously easy way, by selling drugs. Surrounded by material possessions, wearing gold and diamond jewelry, and always dressed to kill, he believed he had *"it"* made. Burglary became a game with potentially rich rewards and rules that were very simple to follow: watch for the rich folk, monitor their comings and goings; call, and if there is no answer then scout the place and, if satisfied that the coast is clear, get in and out as fast as possible.

Such was the scenario the night he broke into the home

of two loving and giving people and killed them. As with most soul and heart injured people, his initial reactions when questioned about his crime were to blame his victims. *"If only they had not returned home so soon after I got there, it wouldn't have been necessary for me to kill them."* In this statement, the absence of conscience for what he did is matched only by his unawareness that he was the *trespasser*, he the *thief* and he the *murderer;* a mindset that granted no rights to the victim but saw them as the reason for his problem. In effect, they had not played the game according to his rules so they became dispensable. They were not recognized as human beings, simply objects - ones that on their own territory were in his way and had to be removed.

In the seven years he was in jail, he accomplished much. He completed college and, with the help of a dedicated minister, gradually made his personal journey to a felt presence of God. At this point when asked what prompted his senseless and murderous assault on two innocent people, he replied,

"My aching heart had turned to stone."

Within the same breath and within the same train of thought, he expressed the song and the lament of his lost inheritance as a child of God. Beginning at conception as an unwanted child, this theft continued throughout his childhood when he was virtually forsaken and abandoned by his parents. It continued through his early childhood and adolescence until it came to a lethal halt. His *song* was the ache in his heart and soul to know, to experience and to feel connected to love, as well as respect for himself and others. The *lament* was what the absence of this life-giving nurturance had done, to first dull and then stamp out all feeling of connection to it. Ultimately, he abandoned not only hope, but belief in its existence. Thus did the people he murdered become for him objects to be dispensed with in the pursuit of theft of a different kind.

His song and lament echoes its resonance and dissonance in the souls of children all over the world. In the past two decades the dissonance has reached a deafening intensity which is having a deadening effect on the soul of society everywhere. In addressing the consequences of this dissonance, society has for the most part focused on modifying the many and various tonalities of its expression. But, as with all songs and laments, one cannot change the tunes without changing the musical score. And the score cannot be written or re-written without the experience at some level of consciousness of the thoughts and feelings that precede it.

Thoughts and feelings are the tonalities of the soul; the forerunners of the behavior that is played out on the stage of life. Thus, in order to modify behavior, we must first know how the thoughts and feelings that preceded it interplayed to create it. My intention in what follows is to draw attention to the almost impossible dilemmas that children are made to cope with at the turn of the 21st Century. That the origins of most of these dilemmas are none of their doing, makes the message of their dysfunctional behavior and violence all the more poignant and urgent of redress. They feel their sense of disconnectedness profoundly and, in my encounters with them, their deepest yearning is always for the possession of their soul and repossession of what they have lost. Instinctively, they know that without this they cannot live in harmony with themselves, their neighbors and the world.

I

Soul, Conscience, and Children

Religion is not an option
or a strictly individual intuition,
but represents the long unfolding,
the collective experience of all humanity,
of the existence of God —
God reflecting himself personally
on the organized sum of thinking beings,
to guarantee a sure result of creation
and to lay down exact laws for humankind's
hesitant activities.

P. Teilhard de Chardin

Truth and non-violence are not possible
without a living belief in God,
meaning a self-existent, all-knowing,
living Force
which inheres in every other force
known to the world and which
depends on none,
and which will live when all other forces
may conceivably perish or cease to act.
I am unable to account for my life
without belief in this all-embracing
living Light.

Mahatma Gandhi

Few could argue that religion plays a central role in the lives and culture of people everywhere; or, that the religious rituals surrounding the major events in people's lives are those that are most remembered and talked about. Indeed, births, marriages and deaths are the threads that weave family histories and often, though not always, strengthen family bonds. But, while the rituals of rites of passage are crucial to our human identity, religion — *at its core* — in its deepest, truest meaning speaks personally to each individual soul. Whatever the name of the religion, the message conveyed is intrinsically the same as all others: that we are spiritual beings as well as physical beings; that for us to know, to touch and to be known and touched by life we must daily search for and be aware of the love that emanates from the same God of creation that we all worship and whom we experience within our souls.

Alas, *soul* is a very over–used word. But, what is it? Has anyone seen soul, has anyone heard soul, tasted soul, or smelt soul? Maybe, and then again, maybe not. However, I venture that everyone has at some time in her or his life *felt* soul. It is said that soul is the repository of feelings and emotions and, thus, the spiritual part of our human nature. It is the very principle of life that comes from creation.[1] If so, it is that which connects us to others, gives conscience it's life and, ultimately, that which ennobles us. Its function then is not only personal, but transpersonal, and finds its expression in reverence and respect for others regardless differences in color, race, religion, perceptions and, indeed, for all creation.

Yet, one has only to be tuned in to the daily news to know that violence is an enormous and hauntingly pervasive problem all over the world:

Within families, between families;

within religions, between religions;

within ethnic groups, between ethnic groups;

within nations, between nations.

Violence thrusts its tentacles deep into the heart and soul of humankind that in agony cries out for love and tolerance to take its place. What is wrong with we who are human? What is it that plays to the keys of destruction rather than creation? Violence perpetrated by children and adolescents — on each other, on parents and family, on other adults, and in many different situations — is particularly vicious. Indeed, all over the world their energies are being squandered in the *slaying* grounds of home, school, neighborhood and, alas, all too often, in the battlefields of the world.

International Law forbids the use of children as combatants. Indeed, recently, the United Nations added a protocol to the *Convention on the Rights of the Child* that recommends 18 as a new minimum age for military service.[2] One wonders, sadly, if it will be any better observed or enforced than the present protocol which recommends 15 as the minimum age for military service. A recent review of soldiers in the ranks of armies in countries where internecine fighting has recently or is currently taking place revealed that a sizable proportion are children. The front ranks, hospital beds and battlefield graves of the armies of poor nations around the world are increasingly filled with boys well below the age of 15 and some as young as 7 or 8 years old.

The era we live in tempts military personnel to co-opt children and violate their innocence. At the same time, as the average age of the global population is sinking, high-tech infantry weapons are being made so light that they are easily shouldered by children. War, industrialization, and migration from the country to the cities have torn at the family and clan ties that traditionally governed conduct in Africa, Asia and

Latin America — all echoing what happened in Europe during the course of the Industrial Revolution. But, whatever the causes, present trends are unmistakable. Estimates of how many children are currently at war range from 50,000 to as high as 200,000 in 24 conflicts. A UNICEF worker in Liberia observed that some boys will do things which grown men cannot stomach. Often, however, they have been prior victims of violence themselves.

A study conducted by *Save The Children Foundation*, the international relief organization, found that boy soldiers had been terrorized by military commanders often by being hung upside-down from trees, or being forced to shoot or slit the throats of their parents. Other methods used to mould a boy soldier are scarcely more subtle: drugs, including marijuana, amphetamines, Valium, amongst others, are handed out. Also, it is said by some professionals and politicians that children do not have belief systems or ideologies, that they are simply sucked up by one side or another and put to the work of killing other human beings who adhere to ideologies different to those of their military masters. The lure of a uniform, shoes, a gun, and other items considered symbols of power and status are considered all that is necessary to co-opt them. As a Pediatrician and a specialist in child development for over three decades, I believe this is a very dangerous concept and one that can only lead to the solidification of violence and war as a way of life. I will explain why in some depth later, but it does flow from scars on the soul and the memories of these scars that are passed from generation to generation in genetic memory.

In the United States, entrenched transgenerational poverty and racial tensions, plus the glorification of violence through films and television, have turned some — but not all

— of the slums of its largest cities into war zones. Yet, America is often regarded by the rest of the world with envy, largely because of the perceived peace within which most of its people live–to say nothing of how it is regarded as the land of milk and honey. Yet, statistics show that for many in the United States of America, this is an illusion.

Juvenile arrests for violent crimes have escalated from 165/100,000 in 1965 to 480/100,000 in 1990 — a 300% increase. Juvenile arrests for murder increased by 85% between 1987 and 1991 and accounted for 17% of *all* violent crime arrests in the USA in 1991.[3] Some of these crimes are committed with unspeakable horror and a degree of sadism that matches the worst in history. For example:

~ A 17 year old boy in Massachusetts was charged with killing his 17 year old girlfriend with a baseball bat — because she would no longer date him.

~ In Atlanta, a 55 year old man who was crippled with Multiple Sclerosis was tortured and stabbed over a period of many hours with kitchen knives and forks; had salt rubbed into his wounds, and was eventually strangled with a rope. His persecutors, and murderers, were three boys, aged 14, 15 and 16.

~ Two teenage girls taking a short cut home through a woods area were attacked, raped and murdered by six males, aged 13 through 16.

~ Three days after killing a 14 year old girl in a botched revenge shooting, an 11 year old male was executed by two gang confederates who were hardly older that himself. He was buried with his Teddy Bear.

~ Two 10 year old boys lured an 8 year old boy and his 5 year old brother to the fourteenth floor of an abandoned apartment building in Chicago. Twice they dangled the 5 year old out a window as punishment for not stealing candy for them. When his 8 year old brother tried to save him, the 10 year olds hit him so hard he let go and his brother dropped to his death.

~An 11 year old was shot by a 12 year old in the school corridor because, as the murderer later said of the victim, "He gave me a funny look."

~ A survey taken in November 1994, reported that 89% of schools in the USA reported violent incidents perpetrated by the students. 25% reported serious injuries and/or death. 79% of these schools reported having police patrols.

No less dramatic are similar trends and occurrences in other Western countries. The United Kingdom and Canada, to mention only two, are other examples. In 1993, two ten year old boys were convicted of the murder of a two year old boy whom they abducted from a shopping mall in Liverpool, England. The detective who broke the case, Phil Roberts of the Liverpool CID, told me that when the verdict was handed down in the Juvenile Court where they were tried, one of the boys cried while the other boy looked across the court room to where Detective Roberts was sitting. Keeping his eyes on him, and without blinking, he clearly sent him two messages:

"If it wasn't for you I wouldn't be here!"

and, *"I'll get my vengeance!"*

Like the protagonist of the *Prologue*, he had no conscience for what he had done, only rage that he had been caught and a hate-filled desire to have his revenge on the one who proved that he committed the crime.

In April of 1996, in California, USA, two eight year old boys and a six year old pummeled a one month old baby with fists and sticks, fracturing the baby's skull, causing severe internal bleeding and probably lifelong disability, if not death, because they said their families didn't get along. Who told them their families didn't get along? Where did this hatred that led to such terrible consequences originate? Where else but in the violent words of their elders. From what they heard, these children took it upon themselves to redress these grievances in a horrendous and vicious manner.

Likewise, on May 1, 1996, a 13-year-old girl was set upon by a group of girls "like a pack of animals" and beaten to death in Corby, Northamptonshire, England.[4] The following day, a headline in London's *The Independent* read, "Girls Get Violent." The article that followed clearly documented the rise in violence perpetrated on females by females, as is shown in *Figure 1.1*.[5]

Figure 1.1

How women are becoming more aggressive

number of women offenders (thousands) — Convictions and cautions — Violence against the person — Burglary — Source: Home Office — 1984 85 86 87 88 89 90 91 92 93 94

*scale — Taking pleasure in violence — Females — Males — 15-17 18-34 35-54 Age — *The index was derived from responses to questions asked of 1,511 people in 1994. Questions asked included: "Do you agree that violence can sometimes be exciting?", "Do you agree that it is acceptable to use physical force to get what you want?". — Source: Socioconsult-MORI/Demos

Research by Ben Summers and Claire Alfree

In her article, Rebecca Fowler states,

"A lot of girls think that to be emancipated one acts like a boy. ...But instead of taking the best traits, like assertiveness, they've gone for the worst: violence. Women have always been portrayed as talented practitioners of evil, but it is as if Lady Macbeth has finally taken up the dagger herself."[6]

In relation to this, recently, there has been a spate of films reinforcing these negative messages to growing and impressionable girls and boys.

One has to ask what has happened to the souls of children.

Why are their consciences dying?

Has the lava of greed and the thirst for money, power, fame and control — the God's worshipped by many of their elders — engulfed their souls and deadened their response to the principles that engender life? Has touch become brutal, and is the very presence of children considered a burdensome distraction by those whose role in their lives should be that of loving nurturance? I think the statistics speak for themselves.

A survey done in 1982 revealed that 83% of parents did not want the children they had. In this regard, things do not appear to have changed much since 1982. In the United States in 1991, 2.7 million children were reported to have been neglected, abused or both.[7] How many other children, having suffered thusly, were not a part of this report? We can surmise that their numbers were anything but few. In this regard, what is most disturbing is that children are the fastest growing segment of the homeless population in the United States of America. In fact, 10% of children in the United States are living in households *not* headed by a natural parent.[8] But what about the millions of children in other countries all over the world, many born into servitude almost from the time they can walk. Others are born to be sold for adoption, and millions of others are abandoned and run the streets of the cities of the world, often bonding in gangs with others who share their fate. These gangs then terrorize.

Figure 1.2 is a brief summary of the violent world of adolescence taken from an article published in the 1991 issue of *Contemporary Pediatrics*.[9] While describing and projecting the consequences of teen violence into the next century, it highlights one of the most urgent health and societal needs of our time; namely, that five million teens *need* but *do not* receive mental health services in the USA alone. If one multiplies this world-wide, the problem becomes one of staggering, if not mind boggling, proportions.

Figure 1.2

THE VIOLENT WORLD OF ADOLESCENCE

If current trends continue, five of every 1,000 young black men turning 15 this year will die in a homicide before they reach the age of 25.

Suicide rates among young people in this country have quadrupled in the past 40 years.

Five million teens need - but do not receive - mental health services.

If current trends continue, about 80% of today's 12-year-olds will be victims of violence during their lifetimes, and half will be victimized two or more times.

One of every 20 persons arrested for a violent crime is less than 15 years old.

47% of the victims of domestic maltreatment are adolescents.

Adolescent females are twice as likely to be raped as older women.

But I have another perspective. Rather than mental health services, I believe that what is needed are *soul* services. Over the past few years *soul* has become the focus of attention for several authors whose numbers can be counted in single digits when it comes to addressing the souls of children. Yet the issues itemized in *Figure 1.2*, as indeed all the fallout from violence, are the consequences of soul injury. Therefore, to not address the soul needs of children will have a chilling, if not catastrophic fallout on the texture and fabric of human society all over the world — and could change it forever.

From the foregoing, it is clear that not only are children and adolescents inflicting violence, they are in no small measure the recipients of it. Multiple causes for this transgenerational cycle of hate and violence are frequently cited: poverty, unemployment, racism, drugs, too easy access to firearms, the media, grandeurization of violence in film and television, and more. Recently, attention has focused on transpersonal issues, i.e., those pertaining to soul. These issues, including everything from the unwanted and abandoned child, to the relationships between children and their parents or parent surrogates, are fraught with conflict. For example, the concept of the "expendable child" is one known well to Pediatricians and Child Psychologists in the West. The expendable child refers to the acting out behavior, as well as the suicidal ideations and attempts, of some children that are the consequence of an unconscious parental wish to be rid of a particular child; not uncommonly, a child with a difficult temperament, one who is handicapped, or otherwise has a chronic long-term illness with a poor prognosis.[10] Almost always the psychosocial history of the perpetrators of such abuse, and indeed of all abuse, reveals that they too have in some way been victimized and, thus, both they and their victims suffer emotional turmoil. While this demonstrates the transgenerational nature of violence and abuse, we have, alas, rarely taken it into account in our treatment of it. Is this because we have not truly seen the connection; or, if having glimpsed it, have we been overcome by its ramifications. If we but touch on even a fraction of the truth in regard to this connection, then we have to see its interconnections to the paths we should be following in turning back this tidal wave of violence by addressing its precursors of anxiety, fear, depression, despair, and most of all, the absence of personal responsibility derived from an absence of personal identity — which itself takes life from a sense of self-worth based on love.

In his book *All God's Children*, published in the fall of 1995, Fox Butterfield speaks to the transgenerational nature of crime. He poignantly suggests that if one wishes to know the cause of violence, one must look to the past.[11] From my perspective, I agree with him.

The United States Government in the 1960s, believing that poverty was the root cause of most social ills, embarked on an ambitious program to eliminate it. This program was called the "War on Poverty." It created and funded many educational, social and health programs — to the tune of billions of dollars — with the expectation that these programs would so improve those who lived in poverty that the outflow would eliminate illiteracy, crime and all the evils that impede the march of society towards Nirvana.

What happened? From the litany of the above statistics, there can be no doubt that the war on poverty failed. Statistically, there is more human suffering and dysfunction in our society today then there was thirty years ago. Data collected in 1992 by the *National Crime Analysis Project of Northeastern University* reported that American killers are getting younger.[12] Homicide arrests per 100,000 males averaged 37.4 for 15 year olds and 57.5 for 16 year olds in 1991, up from 11.8 and 22.4 just six years previously. Even 13 and 14 year olds were more likely to be arrested for murder than men in their 50's. A key concern was, and remains so today, that the victims of minors were often other minors.

Where have we gone wrong? What are we missing
as an essential factor
in the healing of individuals and of society?

Could it be that materialism has overcome not only society in the United States, but world-wide, and drowned out the spiritual essence of whom we really are? And is society, as

Figure 1.3

Factors In Adolescent Violence

Internal Predisposing Factors	External Predisposing Factors
~Age 15+	~Poverty
~Male Sex	~Bias
~Minority status	~Poor schools
~Asynchronous puberty	~High unemployment rates
~Lack of future sense	~Weakened family structures
~Feelings of invulnerability	~Authoritarian, abusive parents
~Need to take risks	~Lack of caring adults
~Need for peer acceptance	~Violent peers and gangs
~Neurologic and psychiatric	~Violence-ridden pop culture
impairments	and media
~Ignorance, illiteracy, lack of skills	

INCREASED VULNERABILITY

Internal Precipitating Factors	External Precipitating Factors
~Drug and alcohol use	~Availability of guns
~Gun possession	~Availability of drugs
~High stress levels	~Traumatic life events:
	loss of home, family
	member, or friend

VIOLENT BEHAVIOR

well as the professionals concerned with easing these problems, wearing blinders and looking only at a part of the prob lem and not at the whole? The evidence certainly would give an affirmative answer to this idea. *Figure 1.3* is an example of this which was published in the October 1991 issue of *Contemporary Pediatrics*.[13] It is very clear and concise and lists most, if not all, of the factors that can be assessed and measured in the life of any child let alone one given to violence. (Fig 1.3) What is missing are the bases upon which the essence of whom we are and whom we become are built. These are *memories*, both individual and transgenerational, and the *many* layered processes we refer to collectively as *consciousness*. In the next chapter, *memory* will be revealed as a kingdom of many mansions which has inherited every territory within the trinity of our bodies, minds and souls. It traverses them with messages of form and function whose purpose is the preservation of our identity and the maintenance of the balance that permits *life*. When these memories are injured or altered from within or from outside, the messages they then convey also become altered; thus, causing alterations in form and function. While these changes can be beneficial, frequently they are not.

But, in either case, it is memory that is the vehicle of life, and consciousness that is it's journey.

Notes

[1] Oxford English Dictionary.

[2] United Nations *Convention on the Rights of the Child* (article 38.4). See also, Mark Frankel, et al., "Boy Soldiers," *Newsweek* (August 14, 1995):44-46.

[3] Material taken from a table published in *Newsweek* (August 2, 1993):43.

[4] Rebecca Fowler, "Girls Get Violent," *The Independent* (May 2, 1996):15.

[5] Taken from a table entitled "How Women Are Becoming More Aggressive: Convictions and Cautions/Taking Pleasure In Violence," *The Independent* (May 2, 1996):15.

[6] Ibid., Fowler, p. 15.

[7] Alwyn Cohall, et al. "Teen Violence," *Contemporary Pediatrics* (September, 1991).

[8] Alwyn Cohall, et al., "Teen Violence," *Contemporary Pediatrics* (October, 1991).

[9] Table taken from Alwyn Cohall, et al., "Teen Violence."

[10] M. Lyon, M. Benoit, P. Getson, T. Walsh, R. O'Donnell, Unpublished Data, 1990. (Quoted originally in *Pediatric Annals,*1992).

[11] Fox Butterfield, *All God's Children: The Bosket Family and The American Tradition Of Violence.* (Knopf: New York, 1995).

[12] National Crime Analysis Project, Northwestern University, 1992.

[13] Table taken from Alwyn Cohall, et al. "Teen Violence."

II

The Power of Memory &
The Journey of
Consciousness

The heavens are telling the glory of God
and the firmament proclaims his handiwork.
There is not a word or a discourse
whose voice is not heard
Through all the earth their voice resounds
and to the ends of the world, their message.

Psalm 19:2-5

The Spirit of the Lord fills the whole world.
It holds all things together and knows
every word spoken by man.

Wisdom 1:7

I am Thou and Thou art I;
and wheresoever Thou art I am there
and I am sown in all;
from whencesoever Thou willest
Thou gatherest Me;
and gathering Me, Thou gatherest Thyself

The Gospel of Eve

Before explaining their roles in the trinity of body, mind and soul, and, thus, of thoughts, feelings and behavior, let me first put memory and consciousness into the context of their peerless meanings and grandeur as sacred mentors of our life. I feel this is necessary given the present controversies and human suffering surrounding what is described as "repressed memory." This has become a major problem for counselors everywhere, but has also become a major reason for litigation against counselors and perceived abusers in the United States.

Responsible counseling demands that clients should essentially be in control of their own journey into healing, with the reassuring and measured guidance of a professional, proficient counselor — much like, but different in its non-directiveness from, the free association that is used in psychoanalysis. Since all counseling is a dialogue of sorts between counselor and the one being counseled, repressed memories can emerge in two major ways. First, the client seeks counseling because of dysfunctional feelings and behavior that are making their lives painful, if not intolerable. Memories of feelings of rejection experienced from the moment of birth, during infancy and childhood that are interfering with their lives can, I believe, by an internal process of transference during counseling, be channeled into avenues of recall of physical and/or sexual abuse, which *may* or *may not* have happened. A climate such as is active presently, wherein abuse of all kinds has high visibility, may serve to heighten the possibility of this happening. Nevertheless, it should be borne in mind that the emotional pain and consequences of rejection, which is abuse in and of itself, can be just as serious as those resulting from physical or sexual abuse. Of course, memories of actual physical and sexual abuse can also be suppressed. Second, a counselor *may* inadvertently give suggestions to a client as to what *may* have happened in their past. These may become imprinted in the client's recall as actual happenings in their lives which, due to their painful overtones, have been repressed in their waking consciousness. The effects of these so-called repressed memories are then perceived as the cause of the client's present dysfunction and disability. Since uncovering the cause of suffering is relief in itself, it is easy to see how these "enabled memories" become the focus of the client's pursuit of resolution. In my opinion, until we have a clearer vision of the dynamic inherent in repressed memory and its phenomena, we should not deny its existence as a powerful progenitor of human dysfunction and suffering. However, we should be *very* cautious about using it at face value in an accusatory way that affects the lives and well-being of people the counselee may identify as their persecutors. Until such time, we should call this phenomenon, *Enabled Memory*.

There is, however, a vast wealth of knowledge about how personal and inter-generational memory serves and drives us through consciousness at all levels of our existence, from it's beginning to it's end. Let me explain. Each gene we inherit from our parents carries a memory which determines and controls not only the color of our eyes, or how we look — that is, our morphism — but also every function within our being. If the memories get damaged or altered, which may happen in a variety of ways, then the activity or function it controls can manifest as *dys-morphism*, *dysfunction* or *disease*. Our immune system operates from memory. Indeed, each time we immunize a child against disease we invite the immune system to create memories of defense against a particular organism so that, if the body temple is later attacked by that organism, the immune system will kick in its memories of how to cope with that organism and eradicate or minimize its effects. In psychological terms, memories of our early experiences play a huge role in how we later perceive ourselves, the world, and all that is external to us.

In his book *The Secret World Of the Unborn Child,* Dr. Verney vividly describes the reactions of the unborn child to the thoughts, feelings and moods of its mother, most of which become imprinted in its memory banks.[1] But, there is more to the imprinting of memories than what happens in the womb. Once having arrived in the external world, recent research has implications for how a mother's actions towards her infant can alter brain chemistry and, thus, its memory functions.[2] For example, if a newborn infant is not held skin-to-skin by its mother within six hours of birth the chemistry of neurotransmission in the Amygdala Nucleus located in the Limbic System — which is that part of the brain that controls emotion and feelings — changes. The Amygdala itself is identified as a determinant of attitude toward the environment and, through its role as coordinator of sensory input from the Neo-Cortex where we do much of our conscious thinking, is responsible for imparting an emotional tone to (thinking) analyses of sensory data. Thus, it is directly concerned with control over aggressive tendencies. The messages it sends through its neural connections results in activation of the Hypothalamus — which is the part of the brain that controls the Autonomic Nervous System. This is where the experiential drama begins because the Autonomic Nervous System controls every function of our body and is the reason why the energy of feelings is felt throughout the body. Thus, from shortly after birth, our later tendency to aggressivity or passivity that derives from feelings, as well as our gut body reactions to threats — whether real or perceived, are stamped in the memory banks of our souls, casting a shadow over or enhancing the primal memory of our beginnings. In terms of what happens to infants born prematurely, and the numerous invasive procedures with which they are assaulted, it is not such a long connection to link the violence of their initial contacts with the outside world — albeit all well intended to save their lives — with subsequent difficulties in learning and adjustment, all well documented in well-designed and carried-out research.

In January 1993, in an article in *Pediatrics,* it was suggested that infants, particularly premature infants, cared for in neonatal intensive care units be touched, held and stroked in a loving reassuring way as often as possible.[3] The intention is to counteract the long-term effects of the somewhat violent nature of the invasive needle and other procedures necessary to save their lives, creating memories of violent feelings which could then influence later perceptions and experiences. Without this intervention these infants are candidates for *Reactive Attachment Disorder of Infancy or Early Childhood* (RADIEC), which results from poor or absent bonding at birth, over or under stimulation, and manifests as emotional and behavioral dysfunction throughout childhood and later life.[4] From my practice, and many years of experience with troubled children, I can attest that the manifestations of RADIEC are very real and almost always present in children who have not been maternally bonded at birth and in the first few months of life. In addition, other recent observations on emotional development in children indicate that the constancy of loving and nurturing contact with the mother in the first six months of life facilitates the subsequent ability to make and maintain healthy human relationships.[5] Does all of this point to validation of the old axiom, "The hand that rocks the cradle, rules the world"? There can be little doubt that it does and, as such, it has a profound message if we have ears to hear in terms of redressing the soul sickness and violence that presently pervades the world in epidemic proportions.

Within this context, one has only to be acquainted with the birthing practices of the last half century in the Western World to perceive their connections and contributions to the memories that later give rise to the symptoms and behaviors associated with being disconnected from love and nurturance. And, being disconnected from love and nurturance is, I believe, the disordered energy at the root of all emotional and behavior disorders, including violence. For example, hospitals, historically centers for caring for the sick, replaced the familiarity of home as places for birthing. While this was well intentioned — to decrease morbidity and mortality — nevertheless, we are now learning that hospital delivery routines have been creating their own morbidity. The practice of turning a newborn infant upside-down on it's arrival from the womb and slapping it on the buttocks to initiate breathing — on the premise this clears respiratory pathways, is hardly a friendly welcome. In uncomplicated deliveries the infant is self-programmed, by memories that go back for eons as part of the birthing process, to initiate its own breathing. It does not need the slap that then resides in its memory as an indicator of a hostile, external world. Subsequent to delivery, infants have often been immediately taken from their mothers and not returned to their arms until hospital schedules allowed.

Further, recent data suggests that 29% of childhood morbidity is due to emotional, behavioral and learning disorders.[6] While not being the whole story, nevertheless, since fear and anxiety result from early negative experiences and are inherent components of emotional, behavioral and learning disorders, it behooves us to make the connection and to pay attention to obstetrical practices which may be contributing to these phenomena. For example, although recent research has shown routine ultrasonography in pregnancy to be meaningless in terms of immediate pregnancy outcome, it continues to be a part of routine prenatal care.[7] Ultrasonography is carried out at a point in pregnancy when cells are migrating from the notochord, which is the primitive nervous system, to their appointed places in the brain. Since ultrasonography slices through tissue in order to get the image, what is this procedure doing to disturb this orderly migration and to cause scrambling and confusion in the pathways of neurotransmission? This and other factors may be interfering with the memories of neural transmission to the point of severe dysfunction, particularly as this affects learning, behavior and emotional stability.

While these perinatal memories as well as those of our early childhood are prime to the engine, there are others that engage its energy to drive it into the consciousness we experience and the personalities we become throughout the journey of our life. Carl Jung referred to these memories as the "collective unconscious," and described them in terms of archetypes. Others, including Dr. Ken Wilber, have described them in the broader terms of the evolution of consciousness throughout time and space.[8]

To understand how these collective memories may operate, let me explore the nature of consciousness itself. In order to be as precise and as clear as one can be about a complex and still very debatable subject, and its impact upon human thoughts, feelings and behavior, I will describe it from two perspectives: "Personal, Individual Consciousness" and "Evolutionary Consciousness" that has developed as a shared property with all of humankind.

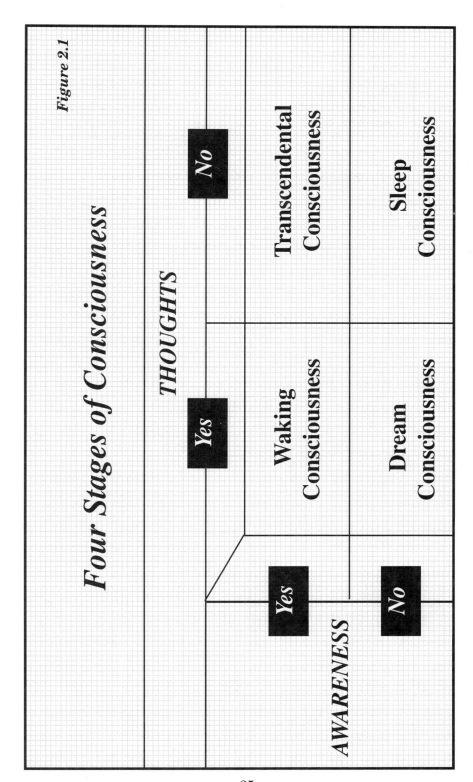

Figure 2.1

Four Stages of Consciousness

Individual consciousness is said to consist of four states (*Figure 2.1*): *Waking, Dream, Sleep* and *Transcendental*. Only in *Waking* consciousness are we aware of our thoughts. Yet, if we have learned anything at all from the great scholars and psychotherapists of this and other centuries, we have to be aware of the profound influence of *Dream, Sleep* and *Transcendental* consciousness on how we perceive reality and, thus, on how we live our lives. In order to understand why, we need to look at the evolution of consciousness itself. In a book about children it is appropriate to compare the evolution of consciousness with the development of a child. By studying the two side-by-side, it is possible to see their striking similarities; thus, making each more comprehensible than if they were described separately. As a pediatrician, I have to say that in general, we pediatricians devote a good part of our endeavors to ensuring as far as we can the guidance and protection necessary through the many phases of a child's development from birth, if not before, to their emergence into independent and, hopefully, positively, self-directed adulthood.

During fetal life and infancy a child is more or less totally dependent on others and is at one with the texture and quality of its environment, and sometimes also at its mercy. As a child grows, this dependency lessens as the central nervous and other systems mature, allowing new skills and new awarenesses to be acquired. This leads to new interactive phenomena with his or her environment, giving new meaning to life and existence at each stage of development. The abundant research, including that which I have quoted, shows beyond doubt that the nature and quality of these interactive phenomena convey messages and create expectations about the world outside of *self* which greatly influence later affect and behavior. In other words, during growth and development, while thoughts and *waking* consciousness change, all experience is stored in the memory banks of body, mind and soul. These memories, though they can be modified, become the bases of belief systems in terms of interpersonal relationships and thus, also of behavior. These experiences likewise have a profound effect, if not also a tutoring role, on *ego* development. This is at the core of how a child perceives him/herself as a separate, independent human being in relation to others. The urge to be free of parental and/or societal regulation and restriction, and to exert one's *ego* independently reaches its peak during adolescence. Alas, it is said of adolescence in the Western world that chronologically it is getting younger but lasting much longer than previously noted. If the tutoring of experience has been nurturing then more than likely the turbulent passage of adolescence will give way sooner rather than later to relative calm. If, however, tutoring has been harsh, punishing and insensitive, the *ego* is much more likely to take on the combativeness associated with low self-esteem. This can and frequently does lead into the whole spectrum of self-destructive behavior, including addictions, as well as dysfunctional, interpersonal behavior, which latter is directed against a world perceived as hostile to self. It is of course when these impasses occur, whether in children, adolescents or adults, that we invite professional counseling to liberate those suffering from their emotional and behavioral prisons. The purpose of professional counseling is, and should always be, to enable the client to grow into new and healthier awarenesses of self and other. This not only permits healing of scars on the soul, but allows tolerance, love and compassion to take up a felt residence in their lives.

Let me now relate this wondrous progress of individual development to those other worlds within our milieu which derive from the evolution of consciousness. They have been described by Carl Jung as the *Collective Unconscious*. Their impact has also been addressed in the marvelous writings about the meaning of myth and dreams of many in the East and West, as well as by several scholars within, if I may coin a word, a psycho-scientific trajectory. Pioneered in this century by scientists such as Robert Ornstein, and spiritual scholars such as Fr. Bede Griffiths, let me briefly outline the hypothesis of Dr. Kenneth Wilber who describes the evolution of consciousness in six stages, always, it seems to me, with reference to its primal source in God.[9] From *Stage 1*, wherein all creation was at one with its creator, humanity journeys its shared and universal consciousness through the phenomena consequent to it's separation from its origin in Creation to its end or *at-one-ment* with its primal source. *Stage 2* relates to the sense of separation humankind experienced when expelled from the Garden of Eden and the fears that accompanied the transition from an existence of loving dependency to one wherein this was not palpably present. Language developed in *Stage 3*, thus allowing description of what was exterior to self by the use of verbal symbols. Language combined with the inner sense of separation from the source of dependent lovingness, which emerged in Stage 2, allowed the concept of blame to form. This was aggrandized during *Stage 4* in which *ego* emerged as a driving force. It also coincided with the rapid development of the neocortex in the human brain whose function, among others, is rational and logical thought. This not only created within the individual a sense of separate, independent existence, but provided the means to rationalize and thus intensify the sense of separation of *self from others*. It is within this frame of reference that humankind can create excuses to insist on its individual autonomy and render violence in thought, word and deed on others whom, by being different, it perceives as threats. *Stage 5* signals a return to *source* and, thus, glimmers of an end to the terrors of being separated from it. It is referred to as *Trans-Personal* consciousness; the awareness that we can reach beyond ourselves to encounter *other* with love and compassion. This hoped for quality for all humanity has always been at the core of personal spiritual experience and all religions. However, for the past several years, this quality has found a home in the tenets of Trans-Personal Psychology. *Stage 5*, with its opening to other, is the prelude to the return to source — bringing consciousness full-circle to its beginnings which occurs in *Stage 6*. Wilber calls this the stage of *Supreme* consciousness, wherein, through meditation and compassion for others, we can experience God. It is in this stage that we also encounter the meaning of angels and saints as messengers of love and of eternal universal energy.

It is believed that we carry within us memories of, and the potential to experience all these levels of consciousness. *Stages 1-4* are mostly experienced within our dream and sleep consciousness from where they influence our waking consciousness. It is *Stage 5* that truly calls us to the journey of being divinely human; the transcendence of self to the realization that *other* is also *I*, and that together we can reach at-one-ment with God.

So when we seek the real cause of violence in our children, teens and, indeed, also in adults, we need to look to the memories in their consciousness that have contributed to it. Further, while it is important to give attention to the variables frequently associated with behavioral dysfunction and violence, it will not be until we penetrate and change the negative energy of hurtful and destructive memories that we will be able to create positive *self* and *other* nurturing consciousness.

Can this change take place? I believe the answer is a resounding, *YES!*

While the messages of the stories and myths about creation and life in all religions inform us of the primal and continuing struggle between good and evil, they also inform us that Life is a journey; the only constant in which is change. These junctions of change offer choices which become the exercise of free will. Whatever choice is made alters the energy deep within our mind, soul and body which then becomes the electrochemical infrastructure of our being and the substrate from which memories are created. Indeed, change and choice are so pervasive that they can actually change the memories within our genes and thus the messages that they carry.[10] If these messages become so scrambled that they can no longer jibe or interact with messages controlled by other genes, then disease and dysfunction will ensue. We call this genetic mutation, and there are countless examples. Sickle Cell Anemia is a good example. To stave off the effects of the Malaria parasite, the genetic codes for hemoglobin of people living in Africa centuries ago mutated so as to change its structure to better resist its destruction by the parasite. Alas, for Africans living in a world and culture no longer challenged by the Malaria parasite to the same degree, this genetic change initially designed to be protective, can pose its own problems in what are described as Sickle Cell Crises. Recently, news of a successful treatment for these effects was made known — Hydroxy Urea. However, as often happens, the effects of the cure can sometimes be as bad as the disease itself. There are many other examples of such changes but the good news is it doesn't always mean that disease and dysfunction will ensue.

This is particularly true of the changes that occur in

our mind and soul as we encounter the stresses of the hills and valleys of our life. The thoughts we think in our waking state of consciousness, influenced as they are by our other states of consciousness – including the memories of our shared universal consciousness, have a profound effect on our feelings and behavior. These in turn control the functioning of the Autonomic Nervous System which is that part of our nervous system that controls every autonomic function of our bodies: breathing, heart rate, intestines, etc. The Autonomic Nervous System interacts with all systems of the body, as well as the Limbic System which controls our emotions. These interchanges become not only whom we are at any particular point in time, but the interfaces between where we are at and where we want and/or choose to go. The exercise of free will to *choose* our path is a tenet of all religions. This is commonly understood and interpreted to mean that despite the dice our familial and inter-generational memories have dealt us, we can somehow become disembodied from their effects in terms of our behavior which, as already described, is in large measure an expression of them. Given all that has been said about the role of memory in our lives, free will makes little sense unless it is put into the context of the religious wisdom that describes *change* as the only constant in the journey of life.

In light of what is known about memory and consciousness, and their imprinting on our neural pathways, particularly those of affect and response, free will cannot be an *un*-conditioned, conscious decision to follow one path or another. On the contrary, behavior is a trajectory pursued and heavily influenced by the memories of many origins. Isn't this, perhaps, the neuropsychological meaning inherent in the statement (quoted more fully in *Chapter V*) from *Gaudium et Spes,* specifically that which says, *"[Man] often does what he would not, and fails to do what he would."* Clearly, this statement implies that the desire to *be* good, to *do* good is frequently over-ruled by energies and maybe other phenomena, the nature of which are not specified by the authors of this statement. Does this make of free will, as presently understood, a nonentity? No, but it needs radical rethinking.

Free will implies *choice;* choices made by exercising one's will. But the psychologist, Rollo May, and others from many disciplines have strongly and convincingly suggested that in a contest between *will* and *imagination*, imagination always predominates.[11] Imagination, influenced as it is by memories and their energies, can leave *will* a wound in the soul of those who try to overcome by its power. If making choices depends more on imagination than it does on will, then choices are fash-ioned more by the interplay of energies that derive from many memories hidden in the trinity of body, mind and soul rather than by conscious effort. When the behavioral manifestations of these energies are destructive to ourselves and to others, changing them must ultimately be a personal experience of *conversion;* but, a conversion that requires an other-than-self intervention. Seldom does this intervention come directly from the Holy Spirit as it did with St. Paul who received conversion instantly while on his way to Damascus to slaughter Chris-tians. Rather, it is "brokered," if you will, from a variety of sources: ministers, counselors, friends, self-help groups, mu-sic and poetry to mention but a few. But whatever the source, in enabling *conversion* to take place, it tracks us back to the roots of our beings which, ultimately, by any other name, is God. It is that feeling of lightness and of rescue of which the Psalmist spoke, *"I will sing a new song to the Lord"* (Ps. 95). It is the "being born again" in the Spirit. And, being born again is not a one time happening but can and does happen many times a day. However, what makes this new birth possible is a change in the energy of the imagination which resides within the soul.

Since the neural pathways of children are developmentally very susceptible to change, it becomes obvious why our attempts to change society and its proclivity to violence should begin with children.

For this to happen will demand an awareness of how what is biological interacts with environment to render the psychological -- an awareness that will inevitably lead to a radical change in how we treat and manage emotional and behavioral disorders. The fast approaching convergence of Neuro and Behavioral Sciences will, I believe, reveal the majesty of memory in the genesis of whom we are. Even more will this convergence reveal how intervention can change energy whose relation to memory is that of servant to mistress. Then will Science at last find common ground with religion which, regardless creed or denomination, has as its core the tenets whereby humanity can liberate its spiritual heritage.

How we may initiate and nurture this transformation will become clear as the reader journeys through the book. However, let me first address another major contributor to child and teen learning and behavioral dysfunction which can lead to failure, anxiety and ultimately violence.

Notes

[1] Thomas Verney, *The Secret Life Of the Unborn Child*.
(Delta Publishing: New York, 1987).

[2] M. A. Hofer. "Relationships As Regulators," *Psychosomatic Medicine* Volume 46 (1984): 183-197.

[3] Marlene S. Goodfriend, "Treatment of Reactive Attachment Disorder of Infants or Early Childhood," *Pediatrics* 91, No. 1 (January, 1993): 139-142.

[4] *Reactive Attachment Disorder of Infancy or Early Childhood (RADIEC):* (A) Markedly disturbed social relatedness in most contexts, beginning before the age of five, as evidenced by either [1] or [2]: [1]-persistent failure to initiate or respond to most social interactions (e.g., in infants, absence of visual tracking and reciprocal play, lack of vocal imitation or playfulness, apathy, little or no spontaneity; at later ages, lack of or little curiosity and social interest); [2]-indiscriminate sociability, e.g., excessive familiarity with relative strangers or making requests and displaying affection. (B) The disturbance in A is not a symptom of either Mental Retardation or a Pervasive Developmental Disorder, such as Autistic Disorder. (C) Grossly pathogenic care, as evidenced by at least one of the following: [1]-persistent disregard of the child's basic emotional needs for comfort, stimulation, and affection. *Examples:* overly harsh punishment by caregiver; consistent neglect by caregiver; [2]-persistent disregard of the child's basic physical needs, including nutrition, adequate housing, and protection from physical danger and assault (including sexual abuse); [3]-repeated change of primary caregiver so that stable attachments are not possible, e.g., frequent changes in foster parents. (D) There is a presumption that the care described in C is responsible for the disturbed behavior in A; this presumption is warranted in the disturbance in A began following the pathogenic care in C. Taken from DSM-IV-R (313.89).

[5] Stanley Greenspan, "Heading Off Problems In Ego Development," *Pediatric News* (September, 1991).

[6] Taken from *Mortality and Morbidity Weekly Reports*. Centers For Disease Control: Atlanta, GA (August 25, 1995).

[7] B. Ewigman, M. LeFevre, J. Hesser, "Randomized Trial of Routine Pre-Natal Ultrasound," *Obstetrics and Gynecology*

(Volume 76, Number 2, 1990).

[8]B. G. Ewigman, J. P. Crane, et al., "Effects of Pre-Natal Ultrasound On Peri-Natal Outcome," *New England Journal of Medicine* 329, 12 (Sept., 1993): 821-887.
[9] Ken Wilber, *A Brief History of Everything.* (Shambhala Publications, Inc.: Boston, MA, 1995).
[10] E. R. Kandel and J. H. Schwartz, "Molecular Biology Of An Elementary Form Of Learning," *Science* 218 (1982):433-443. E. R. Kandel, "Psychotherapy and the Single Synapse," *New England Journal of Medicine* 301 (1979): 1028-1037.
[11] Rollo May, *Love and Will.* (W.W. Norton & Co.: New York, 1969).

III

The Environment Laments For Children

For all men were by nature foolish
who were in ignorance of God,
and who from the good things seen
did not succeed in knowing him who is,
and from studying the works
did not discern the artisan;...

For from the greatness
of the beauty of created things
their original author, by analogy, is seen.
But yet, for these the blame is less;
For they indeed have gone astray perhaps,
though they seek God and wish to find him.
For they search busily among his works,
but are distracted by what they see,
because the things seen are fair.
But again, not even these are pardonable.
For if they so far exceeded in knowledge
that they could speculate about the world,
how did they not more quickly find its Lord?

Book of Wisdom 13:1, 8-9.

The Age of Nations is past,
the task before us now,
if we would not perish,
is to build the earth.

P. Teilhard de Chardin

Over the last two decades there has been an explosion to the point of a current epidemic in learning and behavioral problems amongst children. Indeed, as the following *figure* shows, 29.5% of all conditions reported as the cause of disability in children 17 years of age and younger in the USA in 1991-92 were classified as Learning Disability.[1] If one adds emotional problems, mental retardation and speech problems, 55.7% of all disability in children can be attributed to these conditions; conditions which have their origins predominantly in disorders of development. Therefore, although all these conditions require therapeutic intervention, nevertheless, in the strict interpretation of the term "medical," implying the need for medical treatment, over half of all disability in children is non-medical in nature.

The causes for this phenomenon are undoubtedly many. On the one hand, as I have already pointed out, birthing practices of the last half-century have contributed in altering the neurotransmissions of messages controlling how children perceive the world external to them, and, thus, their own feelings and emotions. However, on the other hand, we cannot discount environmental factors in many diverse parameters. The air we breathe, the water we drink, the food that we eat are loaded with toxins. The evidence is overwhelming and the yet-to-be seriously heeded fallout, tragic.

On the occasion when she accepted the 1995 Albert Schweitzer Peace Prize, Dr. Lita Heiding entitled her acceptance speech:

"Friends of the Earth, Fellow Passengers On Board the Spaceship 'Planet Earth',
Our Planet Is Dying. Mankind Is In Danger."

CONDITION	NUMBER*	%
Learning Disability	1,435,000	29.5
Speech Problems	634,000	13.1
Mental Retardation	331,000	6.8
Mental or Emotional Problem or Disorder	305,000	6.03
Subtotal	*2,705,000*	*55.7*
All Others	2,153,000	44.3
Total	*4,858,000*	*100.0*

*In Thousands

Figure 3.1

She observed that even if wars between nations and within nations stopped, and there was a lasting cease-fire, another war would continue. This is a silent war, one that many ignore and pretend is not existing. This is the true third world war, and it is going on all over the planet – twenty-four hours a day, and no one has the power nor means of escape from it. It is more frightening than any other war has ever been because, for the first time in history, all life is threatened — from the smallest microbe to plants, animals and humankind. And, humankind itself is leading this war against nature, against creation, and against all life on Earth. This war is not fought with weapons, but for money. Industry is drenching the Earth with toxins, chemicals, pharmaceutical fertilizers, pesticides, and the fallout of nuclear power. The contamination continues through data technology and gene technology. In so doing, it is changing the *very core of species specific* cellular structure and function. For example, in Norway, experiments to replace human DNA with mouse DNA as a treatment for cancer is already underway.

Communities that have for generations sustained themselves from nature's gifts in their immediate environments now find themselves being poisoned by industrial effluents. Promised a good life from the income and business the industrial products would engender, communities learned – often the tragic way — that the opposite was true. The Minamataa catastrophe in Japan where, following the arrival of industry in the 1940s, almost an entire generation was polluted, sickened and disabled by mercury let out into the surrounding waters, is a prototype. Absorbed by the fish, which for centuries had been the staple in their diets, this in turn poisoned the human inhabitants. The tragedy at Bhopal, India is another example of a community destroyed by the empty promises of a better life through industry that manufactures poison. The fallout from the Chernobyl nuclear disaster in Soviet Russia twelve years ago reached to every corner of the world. In Europe, milk and milk products were contaminated as a result of the radio-active contamination of the grass ingested by dairy herds, and children are heavy consumers of milk. Further, in a letter to London's *The Independent* on April 13, 1996, Richard Branhall of the Low Level Radiation Campaign in Britain stated that the full picture of health detriment will take years to emerge. He stated that official perception of health hazards from man made isotopes err by a factor of as much as 1,000 and maybe more. Meanwhile, and most immediately disturbing is the fact that not only has there been an increase in Thyroid cancer in adults in Europe and North America, but this has been accom-panied by an increase in Hypo-Thyroidism in newborn infants from doses of radioactive iodine that were from 1,000 - 10,000 times smaller than they were in Soviet Russia at the time of the disaster. Hypo-Thyroidism in newborn infants means that throughout intrauterine development, the fetus is subjected to the pervasive effects of deficiency of its thyroid hormones. Although Replacement Therapy can be given after birth, one has to wonder if this catch-up after the fact can ever compen-sate for what has been lost. Likewise, in a newscast on BBC Television in late April, 1996, it was reported that the sheep in Wales are still showing high levels of radioactivity. This radioactivity, derived from the ingredients in the grass the sheep feed on, was deposited there by the winds carrying them from Chernobyl. Lamb is a staple meat in all parts of the United Kingdom and may, in the long run, be far more hazardous to the health and well-being of the population than the BSE (*Bo-vine Spongiform Encephalopathy*) in cattle that has caused, as Michael Haseltine, Deputy Prime Minister, recently stated, the most serious political crisis ever in England.

Indeed, the environment has been so manipulated that it is now almost impossible to purchase any food that is pure. A recent report concerning nutrition suggested that to obtain the same nutrients in one bowl of spinach grown in 1940, an individual would now have to consume 75 bowls. Most of our vegetables travel long distances before we purchase them, sprayed with preservatives that are, in fact, contaminants. Manipulation of form and taste has progressed to a point where giving anyone under the age of forty a real, naturally grown tomato the reaction will be, "But it doesn't look or taste like a tomato." Furthermore, the rise in obesity amongst children has recently been attributed in part to the hormones in the food they eat. This is not surprising given that in North America children, in general, consume large amounts of bread and milk; products that from their seeds are saturated with them — grain products that grow from soil treated with hormone changing pesticides and milk and milk products from cows actually given hormones in their feed. It has been said that bread contains everything but flour.

At the World Conference On Environmental Issues, held in Rio de Janeiro in 1992, the Director General of UNESCO, Federico Major y Sargasso, declared, "By abuse of natural resources, Man is on the threshold of exterminating all life on Earth - including humankind itself."

Who is listening?

Certainly not those who are getting rich from the poisons they are showering on creation. But their end will undoubtedly prove to be not unlike the man who died of hunger, cursed by his wish that everything he touched would turn to gold. It did, including his food.

We live in an era which I have labeled, "Instant Mania." In our quest to possess, have or produce everything the minute we think of it, we have abrogated our perspective on history and the future. This instant mania has overflowed into the mind-set of those who manufacture the poisons that are killing us. Little if any thought is being given to the kind of environment they are bequeathing to future generations. This was brought home forcibly to my attention one evening several summers ago. I was sitting on the porch of my mountain home enjoying the beauty of the scene — birds fluttering here and there, their songs combined with the hum of the insects busy about their lives and their role in creation, as well as the searches they make for nurturance and survival. As I marveled at the joy of it all, my eyes came back to the field lying straight ahead of me. The stately rows of corn were about four feet tall, growing rapidly now to give the gifts of their fruit. My eyes traveled down through the symmetrical rows to the ground from which they sprang. There wasn't a weed or any other form of plant life to be seen anywhere. Hardly believing what I was seeing, with all of its implications, I walked over to the field and down the avenues between the aisles of corn. On rare occasions I would see a mustard weed struggling for its life, stunted, with few leaves and only one or two of its usually marvelous yellow blossoms. "My God," I said out loud. "What are these farmers doing to the land that has since recorded history been so kind to them?" The answer, of course, is all too dreadfully obvious. In order to increase their yield of winter feed for their dairy cattle, they spray the earth with poisons; in this case, with Atrazine, a killer of all plant life except corn which is genetically resistant to its killing effects. In rapid succession my thoughts went through the food chain of that corn. Once absorbed, when the corn is mulched as feed for the cattle, it goes through their systems and then through their milk and the products made from it, into the bodies of all who consume them.

What one must ask is the causative role of these poisons and the hormones fed to the cattle that have developed BSE, or Mad Cow Disease. Following a report released on March 22, 1996, that speculated on the possibility of a connection between this disease in cows and the deadly Crutzfeldt-Jakob disease in humans, the British Government was faced with the possibility of having to exterminate the entire population of cows in the United Kingdom. By March 24, 1996, all but two European countries had banned British beef and nations as far away as Singapore and New Zealand had done the same, cutting off trade that earns Britain $780 million a year. The domino effect of this on the British economy could be potentially catastrophic. It should, however, serve as a lightening rod to other consequences resulting from the mindless manipulation of the environment and of all creation for the purpose of short-term gain.

Knowledge that the Earth is steadily being poisoned is no recent discovery. In 1947, almost a half century ago the Norwegian explorer, Thor Heyderhal, discovered lumps of oil of various sizes in the Pacific Ocean. Realizing they were signs of pollution of the seas, he informed NATO of his findings. Not understanding the implications, those with whom he talked nodded and did nothing. In 1962, Dr. Rachel Carson's book *The Silent Spring,* stampeded its message onto the world stage.[2] Initially observing that in the locale where she lived birds of all species suddenly disappeared, she discovered that a poisonous pesticide had been sprayed along the hedgerows in the roads adjacent to her home. As a biologist, she was intrigued and thus, began research — the results and message of which were rendered to the world in her book. I remember well the stir that her message caused. I also remember very well the occasion when she was questioned by many high powered executives who were in the business of making pesticides during a special television program. The quiet, restrained, focused, and well-informed answers this great, tough and gentle woman gave to the verbal onslaughts thrust upon her greatly moved and impressed me. It was obvious then that the forces of gain had joined with those of preservation, and that gain had the stranglehold. Dr. Carson died not too long afterwards of cancer. Was this caused by the same pesticides that silenced the bird songs along her hedges? It is possible, but

Who, if anyone, was listening?

Well, in 1972, the United Nations put on a conference in Stockholm to discuss the issues Dr. Carson had raised. After hearing of the disasters that lay ahead if a stop was not put to the manufacture of earth and creation poisons such as climate changes, depletion of the ozone layer and other phenomena, the 111 nations present signed what came to be known as "The Stockholm Declaration." Then they went home, and did nothing of lasting consequence. As Dr. Heiding observes, this was not due to inertia; rather, to the pressures put on Governments by the multi-national corporations that manufacture the poisons. With a world that has 10 million chemicals registered in the Chemical Abstract Service, it seems an anachronism that in the United Nations' own *International Register For Potential Toxic Chemicals,* only a few of these are deemed to be dangerous. Who makes these determinations? Who is controlling them?

In a conversation that Dr. Heiding had with the President of the International Organization of Chemical Manufacturers, she was told by him: "You cannot stop us. Do you really believe that politicians are ruling the world? If so, you are wrong. We are ruling the world because we have the money." She asked him, "What will you do if people stop buying your product?" "Well, that is different," he replied. "We must produce something that people will buy." Herein lies the answer to the dilemma. Margaret Mead, the American anthropologist, said, "Never doubt that a small group of thoughtful, committed citizens can change the world. Indeed, it's the only thing that ever has."

Perhaps a recent report by the Environmental Protection Agency (EPA) on the long term effects of Dioxin may finally get the attention of those who have the power to stop this rape and murder of the Earth.[3] The report suggests that, as a hormone disturbing chemical, Dioxin is probably causing major fertility problems in all species, as well as cancer and other diseases. This report was followed by another one published in the *British Medical Journal* in February, 1996.[4] While it is common knowledge that over the past few years human sperm counts have been dropping, researchers in Edinburgh, Scotland reported that men born after 1970 have sperm counts 25% lower than those born previous to 1959 – an average decline of 2.1% per year. A 1995 study of Parisians found an identical male infertility decline over the past 20 years. And, in the most comprehensive analysis of all, covering 15,000 men from 21 countries, Danish scientists discovered an alarming plunge of nearly 50% in average sperm counts over the past half-century.[5] Not only are sperm counts dropping but the quality of the sperm – the percentage of healthy, vigorous cells versus malformed, sluggish ones – appears to be in serious decline as well.

In a recently published and widely touted book, *Our Stolen Future,* the authors claim that a wide range of reproduction related ills may be caused by chemical pollutants in the environment.[6] Chief among these are DDT, some forms of Dioxin, and PCBs, as well as a number of other synthetic substances. They postulate that exposure to even small traces of these chemicals in the womb can interfere with proper development of the reproductive system, leading to serious consequences years, decades and maybe even centuries later. The rise in male infertility is just a part of the problem, say the authors. These pollutants may also be responsible for the rise in breast cancer and other cancers, as well as aberrant mating behavior and genital malformation in animals. This is reinforced by a study done by a zoologist at the Wildlife Fund.[7] She states that the young of sixteen predator species, including fish, reptiles and mammals, were failing to survive to adulthood and couldn't reproduce if they did survive. All these animals ate fish from the Great Lakes of North America which are contaminated with hormone changing chemicals.[8] Worse still, when this zoologist looked at human epidemiological studies it suggested that human fetal exposure to such chemicals could produce disorders affecting behavior, immune system functioning, memory and learning. From my many years of experience as a Pediatrician, I have no doubt in my mind that her observations are correct.

Yet, in July of 1995, "The Contract With America," proposed by the Republican Party of the United States Congress, suggested major cutbacks for the EPA. This would allow mercury, lead, and other heavy metals and toxins to flow from industrial waste into the Great Lakes which are already poisoned almost beyond their ability to sustain the fish and other life within their waters. And, if this wasn't bad enough, add to it the first steps it proposes to take toward selling-off the American national heritage. In 1864, President Abraham Lincoln signed legislation to preserve Yosemite Valley for all time. Since then 623 million acres of ecologically significant lands have been set aside to be held in sacred trust for *all generations*. In 1995, the U.S. Congress, in its contract *on* America, drew up legislation that would sell-off national forests to be logged, wildlife refuges to be drilled for oil and gas, and national parks to be developed by private investors. The terrible fallout from these further assaults on the natural environment can only do more damage to our already impaired children - leading not only to an escalation in learning and behavioral disorders, but in other more immediate life threatening conditions as well.

And then, when these children, whose normal development has been scrambled, hit the streets in despair and terrorize the populace — what will be the response?

More prisons?

Probably!

I believe that these poisons are causing profound changes in the neural pathways of children that control and monitor cognition and other learning modalities. Perusal of the evaluations I conduct for children referred to me because of learning and behavioral difficulties — which include a neuro-developmental assessment — leave no doubt of the increasing pervasiveness of these problems. This assessment, which initially is very basic, includes the status of neuro-maturation in several parameters; Temporal Sequential Memory – the ability to organize same into a meaningful whole; Visual Perceptual Function; short and long-term memory; and other parameters of neural function whose integrity is essential for learning. My findings show beyond doubt that of the children referred to me most, if not all, have such profound problems in these parameters that they cannot function as expected in the classroom. For example, *Figures 3.2* and *3.3* show the forms and shapes used for initial screening of Visual/Perceptual/ Motor function. Also, the ages at which a child should be able to reproduce these forms more or less perfectly, as well as what a 14 year old boy, who was referred because of behavioral problems, did with them. *Figure 3.2* shows what he did by direct copying. It is obvious that he is beginning to fail at the 7 year old level, fails at the 8 and 9 year old level and by the 9 and 10 year old level, gets rattled and retreats to the bottom of the page. His anxiety almost jumps out at you. In *Figure 3.3*, copying from memory, he clearly fails at the five year level — the bottom of the triangle not being even, thus indicating not only Visual Perceptual Motor dysfunction but, also, problems with short-term memory.

Now imagine that you are this 14 year old boy sitting in a classroom where all learning has as its basis the interpretation of symbols. Clearly, one's mind and brain is not able to process form and structure, therefore much that is required of this student cannot be processed or reproduced as expected. Does this cause *anxiety*? You bet it does. Does this cause *fear* of consequences for non-performance? You bet it does. Does this cause a sense of failure and powerlessness? You bet it does. Does this make the young man or woman cut and run? You bet it does!

None of us, infant, child or adult, can live with a sense of failure and powerlessness without some part of our being cracking wide open. This breakage occurs at the point of the weakest links in our genetic and experiential memories and is facilitated by the burdens put on the Autonomic Nervous System by these negative energies which respond by communi-

Figure 3.2

Forms To Copy For The Screening Of
Visual Perceptual-Motor Function

AGE (Years)	FORMS FOR DIRECT COPYING			
5				
6				
7				
8				
9-10				
11-12+				

Figure 3.3

Forms To Copy For The Screening Of
Visual Perceptual-Motor Function

AGE (Years)	COPYING FROM MEMORY (10 Second Exposure)
5	
6	
7	
8	
9-10	
11-12+	

cating messages of imbalance to all systems and functions of the body it controls. The dynamics of these interactions will be described more fully in the next chapter but children who endure the absence of love and loving discipline in their homes and/or have to deal with a daily dose of anxiety and personal failure in the classroom, become alienated from all that engulfs them. The isolation they endure leads to the loss of the most precious thing any of us can have which is a healthy sense of our own unique identity. Thoughts and feelings about *whom* they are, *where* they come from, and *where* they are going become a maze that makes no sense and, at this point, they become scarred at the deepest level of their beings — their souls.

I also believe that the increase in attention disorders, often referred to generically as Attention Deficit Disorder (ADD) with or without Hyperactivity (ADD-H), derives in significant proportions from the scenarios I have just described. It is estimated that over 2 million children in the USA are classified — I would say, "labeled" — as having ADD-H. I have long believed that this is a garbage diagnosis. It compares with giving someone a "diagnosis" of fever without reference to its cause. Like fever, ADD-H is a symptom and one should not embark on its treatment without reference to its cause, no more than one would conscientiously embark on treating a fever without first identifying its cause. Both have multiple causes. In fact, if one examines just the major symptoms of anxiety, it is clear that any combination of them would lead to the dysfunctional behaviors cited as "symptoms" of ADD-H.[9] Thus, what needs to be addressed is the trauma that is causing the problem.

So when we look at the statistics listed in *Figure 3.4,* let us remember that children and teens are hurting, and the abuse, neglect and violence that has been and continues to be

THE AGONY OF CHILDREN	
Number of children ages 10-18 in the United States	31,000,000
Average number of children who suffer a violent death from child abuse every year in The United States	1,383
Percentage of child deaths that involved firearms	10%
Number of teens who commit suicide every day	11
Number of suicides per 100,000 teens in 1960	3.6
Number of teen suicides per 100,000 today	11.3
Rank of suicide as a cause of death among children and teens	3rd
Number of teens who were murdered last year	4,173

Rate of death out of 100,000 by homicide-
    for young white men
    for young black men
	
	11.5
	101.8

Number of teens who are homeless	1,500,000
Number of children orphaned by A.I.D.S.	60,000

Figure 3.4

Figure taken from the 1992 Newsletter of the National Association of Police Officers

perpetrated on them is coming back to us as their violence. It is the loudest cry for help the world has ever known. It is a primal scream that also cuts across addictions of all kinds and other means of escape, yelling:

"Let me out of my prisons."

The manifestations of these prisons can often be subsumed in three diagnostic categories: Post-Traumatic Stress Syndrome, Reactive Attachment Disorder in Infants & Early Childhood and Dysautonomia.[10] The symptoms are many and varied, but all are due to the deep fear, anxiety and depression that ensues from the trauma of physical, emotional and spiritual deprivation and violence. To this must now be added the violence that the poisons in our environment are inflicting on normal development from conception onwards; they are in fact diverting the normal development of many neural pathways including those of cognition, awareness of conscience and behavioral responses.

Given the evidence, it is not too much to assert that the curricula taught in our schools — and the manner of its presentation — no longer matches the ability of many children to adequately respond to them.

This has been recently corroborated by a report filed by the United States Industrial Commission on Training and Education which found that among High School graduates, only a few could read and write to the level required for on-the-job training. Commenting on this report, Louis Gerstner, Chief of IBM, in March of 1996 said, "What is killing us (as an industry) is having to teach them (High School graduates) to read, compute..., and to think." While it is anachronistic to hold a High School diploma while not being able to read and write, and there are many who do not have these basic skills, concern at the situation has called for a halt to the "social promotion" that creates it. While adding his voice to the chorus, President Clinton in late March, 1996, called for parents and teachers to demand the best efforts of the children.

Laudable and appropriate though this may be, if one doesn't have the hardware to respond to the software, nothing can change.

These changes will not occur until we put our hand to the plough that will cut a different road for humankind to prosper, let alone grow and survive.

In his book *Earth In The Balance*, published before he became Vice President of the United States, Al Gore said,

> By failing to provide world leadership in the aftermath of the victory over communism and in the face of the assault by civilization on the global environment, the United States is once again inviting a descent toward chaos. History is change, and change is a relentless, driving force. Now that the human community has developed

into a truly global community, we have a choice; either we search for the means to steer the changes shaping our new common history or we will be steered by them - randomly and chaotically. Either we move toward the light or we move toward the darkness.[11]

In an equally profound statement published in London's *The Independent* on May 6, 1996, Tom Burke, former Director of *Friends of the Earth*, stated that the Earth now needs smarter friends than previously because the successes of the past 25 years have been mere tactical victories in a long retreat for the environment. Specifically, Burke stated,

> The brutal truth about the politics of the environment is that all the successes of the past quarter century have been no more than tactical victories in the long retreat for the environment in the face of inexorable pressure from a rising population with rising income that it spends unwisely.
>
> The agenda of the easy politics is very familiar: air and water quality; waste from contaminated land; endangered species, chemicals and radioactivity. The successes in tackling these issues have been real, especially in the West, and they continue. The new environmental agenda is unfamiliar: food security; fish stocks; water availability; forests; climate change, transport policy. These are the issues that will have to be tackled successfully in the next 25 years if our grandchildren are to inherit prospects as good as we did.
>
> Just how difficult this will be is well illustrated by some recent events. The recent conversion of the US Secretary of State, Warren Christopher, to the environmental cause has been driven in a large part by his enforced understanding that there can be no lasting peace in the Middle East without an agreement among the warring parties about how to distribute the region's scarce water resources in the face of its burgeoning population.
>
> ... As we face the more difficult choices of the future (Friends of the Earth) will need to learn to cooperate as well as confront, to solve as well as to shout, while losing none of its dynamic aggression. The earth that needed its friends 25 years ago needs them even more today, but

they need to be smarter, more confident, more mature and, above all, more committed than ever.[12]

Meanwhile, the cumulative effect of these and other assaults on body, mind and soul is creating enormous *stress* for our children.

Notes

[1] These are the most recent years for which complete data is available. The data presented was originally published in *Mortality and Morbidity Weekly Reports*. Atlanta, GA: Center for Disease Control:, (August 25, 1995):612.

[2] Rachel Carson. *The Silent Spring*. (Houghton Mifflin: New York, 1962). 1994. Introduction by Vice President Al Gore.

[3] Linda Birnbaum, "Developmental Effects of Dioxins." *Environmental Health Perspectives*, 103, Supplement No. 7, (1995); also, R. Reigart and S. Cummins, "Limit Hormone-Disrupting Chemical Exposure." *AAP News* (April, 1996).

[4] See three articles from the February 24, 1996 issue of the *British Medical Journal*, v312, n7029: D. M. de Kretsner, "Declining Sperm Counts: Environmental Chemicals May Be To Blame" (p. 457); S. Irvine, et. al., "Evidence of Deteriorating Semen Quality in the United Kingdom: Birth Cohort Study in 577 Men in Scotland Over 11 Years" (p. 467-470); and, L. Bujan, et. al., "Time Series Analysis of Sperm Concentration In Fertile Men in Toulouse, France, Between 1977 and 1992" (p. 471-472).

[5] Lemonick, Michael D., "What's Wrong With Our Sperm?" *Time* (March 18, 1996):78-79.

[6] Theo Colborn. *Our Stolen Future*. (Dutton: New York, 1996).

[7] Wildlife Fund Study

[8] "Fish In The Great Lakes," *Time* (September 19, 1994).

[9] The following represent some of the numerous symptoms of Anxiety: light-headedness, faintness or dizzy spells; sensation of rubbery or "jelly" legs; feeling off balance or unsteady as if about to fall; difficulty in getting breath or overbreathing; skipping or racing of the heart; chest pain or pressure; smothering or choking sensation or lump in throat; tingling or numbness in parts of the body; hot flashes or cold chills; nausea or stomach problems; episodes of diarrhea; headaches or pains in neck or head; feeling tired, weak, and exhausted easily; spells of increased sensitivity to sound, light or touch; bouts of excessive sweating; feelings that surroundings are strange, unreal, foggy, or detached; feeling outside or detached from part or all of your body or a floating feeling; worry about your health to much; feeling you are

loosing control or going insane; having a fear that you are dying or that something terrible is about to happen; shaking or trembling; unexpected waves of depression occurring with little or no provocation; emotions and moods going up and down a lot in response to changes around you; being dependent on others; having to repeat the same action in a ritual; difficulty in falling asleep; waking up in the middle of the night or restless sleep; recurrent words or thoughts that persistently intrude on your mind and are hard to get rid of; tension and inability to relax; mouth drier than usual; worried, preoccupied; nervous, jittery, restless; afraid, fearful; tense, uptight; shaky inside or out; fluttery stomach; warm all over; sweaty palms; tremor in hands or legs.

[10] *Post-Traumatic Stress Disorder:* A. The person has experienced an event that is outside the range of usual human experience and that would be markedly distressing to almost anyone, e.g., serious threat to one's life or physical integrity; serious threat or harm to one's children, spouse, or other close relatives and friends; sudden destruction of one's home or community; or seeing another person who has recently been, or is being, seriously injured or killed as the result of an accident or physical violence. B. The traumatic event is persistently reexperienced in at least one of the following ways: (1) recurrent and intrusive distressing recollections of the event (in young children, repetitive play in which themes or aspects of the trauma are expressed); (2) recurrent distressing dreams of the event; (3) sudden acting or feeling as if the traumatic event were recurring (includes a sense of reliving the experience, illusions, hallucinations, and dissociative [flashback] episodes, even those that occur upon waking or when intoxicated); (4) intense psychological distress at exposure to events that symbolize or resemble an aspect of the traumatic event, including anniversaries of the trauma. C. Persistent avoidance of stimuli associated with the trauma or numbing of general responsiveness (not present before the trauma), as indicated by at least three of the following: (1) efforts to avoid thoughts or feelings associated with the trauma; (2) efforts to avoid activities or situations that arouse recollections of the trauma; (3) inability to recall an important aspect of the trauma (psychogenic amnesia); (4) markedly diminished interest in significant activities (in young children, loss of recently acquired developmental skills such as toilet training or language skills); (5) feeling of detachment or estrangement from others; (6) re-

stricted range of affect, e.g., unable to have loving feelings; (7) sense of a foreshortened future, e.g., does not expect to have a career, marriage, or children, or a long life. D. Persistent symptoms of increased arousal (not present before the trauma), as indicated by at least two of the following: (1) difficulty falling or staying asleep; (2) irritability or outbursts of anger; (3) difficulty concentrating; (4) hypervigilance; (5) exaggerated startle response; (6) physiological reactivity upon exposure to events that symbolize or resemble an aspect of the traumatic event (e.g., a woman who was raped in an elevator breaks out in a sweat when entering an elevator). E. Duration of the disturbance (symptoms in B, C, and D) of at least one month.

[11] Gore, Al. *Earth In The Balance: Ecology of the Human Spirit*. (Penguin Books: New York, 1992, 1993): 172-173.
[12] Burke, Tom. "The Earth Now Needs Smarter Friends," *The Independent* (May 6, 1996):15.

IV

Stress and Children

The makers of images dwell with us still.
We must listen to their speech,
re-learn their songs.
Recharge the psychic interspace
of our dying age.
Or live dumb and blind,
devoid of old song —
divorced from the great dreams
of the magical and fearful
universe.

"Lament of the Images"
An African Elegy
Ben Okri

If the doors of perception were cleansed,
everything would appear to humankind
- as it is - infinite.

William Blake

I have put duality away. I have seen the two
worlds are one;
one I seek, one I know, one I see, one I call.
(S)he is the first. (S)he is the last.
(S)he is the outward. (S)he is the inward.

Rumi
Persian Poet

Given the many and varied skills of this generation, nevertheless, from what has already been presented, it is obvious that a large proportion of children are being asked to function in ways that are becoming increasingly difficult for them. The tensions created by the discrepancies between expectations and performance causes profound anxiety and depression which inevitably leads to stress — which is often shared by their parents or surrogates and teachers. Yet, the present regard for the illiteracy and poor performance of children and young adults may pale in the face of the confusion that will undoubtedly ensue from a recently published report that, at first acquaintance, may lead one to draw polar opposite conclusions. A historical review of I.Q. scores conducted by James R. Flynn, a political philosopher at the University of Otago in New Zealand, revealed that there have been massive gains in I.Q. scores in all technologically developed nations since the inception of I.Q. scores at the turn of this century.[1] Simplistically explained, and when juxtaposed with the large number of children having problems, this could mean either of two things, or a combination of both. First, that a large fraction of today's children are gifted in comparison to previous years and that an equally large portion of children have problems — a happening that would turn the presently accepted Bell Curve of distribution of intelligence literally upside-down – or that almost half of white Americans tested during World War I had I.Q.s so low they lacked the intellectual capacity to even understand the basic rules of baseball. But, as Flynn himself contends, it is more than likely that the gains in I.Q. are too large to represent *true* intelligence.

What, one may ask, is *true* intelligence? I, and others, have long believed that the nature of intelligence is so multifaceted that it almost defies definition. In a book entitled

Emotional Intelligence, published in October, 1995, Dr. Daniel Goleman asserts for all of us, not just for those of us who have long doubted the value of I.Q. tests, that our view of intelligence is far too narrow.[2] Drawing on ground-breaking brain and behavioral research, some of which is referred to in this manuscript, Goleman recounts the factors at work when people of high I.Q. flounder and those of modest I.Q. do well. These factors add up to a different way of being smart, one he terms "emotional intelligence." This intelligence includes self-awareness and impulse control, self-motivation, persistence, all combined with zeal, empathy and social deftness. Lack of emotional intelligence can sabotage the intellect, ruin careers and wreck homes and marriages. The greatest toll is on children for whom risk includes not only fear and depression, but all manner of behavioral dysfunction culminating in school failure, aggressiveness and violence. So, while innate wisdom and countless recent articles instruct us on the value of teaching children — *from birth on* — the gifts of behavioral learning that derive from emotional lessons, at present little or none of this is being generally applied. It is becoming increasingly apparent that all experience creates memories of response in our neural pathways and soul that "click in" throughout our lives and that the energy of these responses can be positive or negative. We also know that if the responses are negative, their energy can be changed through simple modalities such as deep-breathing and positive self-talk. These and other modalities to be described later, can be used to teach children self-awareness, self-control, respect for others and, above all, personal responsibility; gifts of learning that would enhance the quality of their lives and ultimately that of society. Alas, they are rarely, if ever, a part of the school curriculum and, yet, they are now needed more than ever since the stress of and on children is likely to continue.

Because of the wrench it has thrown into the belief, held for almost a century, that intelligence can be measured by I.Q. tests, the fierce debates that will swirl around what has now come to be known as the *Flynn Report,* could likely further divert our attention from applying what we know can help children cope with the conflicts of life. While intruding once again on the ever contentious arguments about the respective roles of nature versus nurture in the genesis and maintenance of intelligence, Flynn's report begs many other questions and comparisons.

At a conference that was called to address these issues, held at Emory University in Atlanta, Georgia in April, 1996, it was pointed out that height, like I.Q., has been rising for decades; not because tallness genes are more common, but because of better nutrition. Dr. Wendy Williams, a psychologist at Yale University, pointed out that much of the I.Q. gain may simply reflect the greater familiarity that today's children have with the sorts of questions posed on the tests. For example, today's cereal boxes and fast food bags are covered with mazes very similar to those presented in I.Q. tests. In the 1930s a child may never have seen a maze before being presented with one on the I.Q. test. It seems clear, she concluded, that I.Q. tests are not measuring innate intelligence but a type of practiced learning and familiarity with the type of test questions used. Moreover, access to television, movies and radio has increased basic vocabulary over the last 30 years. Action packed video games, once relegated to arcades and shopping malls, are now a part of almost every home. They demand navigation through a two-dimensional representation of a 3-D space. Mental paper folding, a prominent feature of the Stanford-Binet I.Q. test, demands the same skill. The spread of these image intense technologies, says Patricia Greenfield of UCLA, could explain the spurt in I.Q. scores.

While these debates rage on, the habit of using I.Q. scores to categorize children will no doubt continue in spite of the fact that it is more clear than ever that their meaning and value as measurements of a child's abilities and potential are questionable and uncertain. Indeed, in her recently published book *The Learning Curve,* Dr. Judith Mishne demonstrates that children's social development must be given paramount importance in order for them to achieve long-term school success.[3] Particularly in the early years, a child's sense of self and his or her ability to trust the environment are the qualities that need to be nurtured *more* than cognitive skills. She concludes that engendering children's independence, self-confidence and, above all, a sense of responsibility for themselves and their studies is at the center of wise and productive learning.

The dilemma is obvious, and is as much a bureaucratic dilemma as it is a personal one for children. I.Q. tests and scores have long been regarded as sacred mentors for teachers, counselors and parents in deciding a child's placement in the educational system, and thus, his or her future. Further, it is not too much to assert that the education system itself, as well as access to higher education, has been based on I.Q. and other scores such as the Scholastic Aptitude Test (SAT). The questions then are (1) What in the final analysis have these tests been measuring? and (2) Has addiction to an infallibility erroneously conferred on them contributed in no small measure to the conflicts children face? Not fitting into a system wherein they are expected to function causes anxiety, fear and depression. This finds expression in behavioral manifestations because of a *felt* disconnectedness from the system, from society and, most of all, from their own souls and sense of self-worth. While there can as yet be no definitive answers to these questions, likewise, there can be no doubt that the conflict for children between whom they are — their inner world, and what is expected of them — the outer world, has created great *stress* for them. And stress is a killer of body, mind and soul.

Briefly stated, *stress* is defined as an imbalance between environmental demands and the coping resources of the individual or, simply stated, an imbalance between the inner and outer worlds. In general, this mis-match or lack of balance manifests in three major ways. First, by causing changes in the normal physiological functions of the body which, if unrelieved, then leads to physical disease. It is estimated that between 85%-90% of all illness is stress induced. Second, subjectively, by causing feelings of distress; and, third, behaviorally, in disturbed personal and interpersonal functioning and performance.

The manner in which the trinity of the body, mind and soul react to stress derives from one of the oldest memories that we carry within us; the physiological response which we call the "Fight" or "Flight" reaction. In the latter part of the 19th Century, Claude Bernard, the great French physiologist, pointed out that the internal environment of living organisms must remain within fairly constant physiological, and, thus, functional parameters despite changes in the external environment. Otherwise, dysfunction and death will ensue. The coordinated physiological processes which maintain this internal stability or Homeostasis is achieved in two ways. First, by a very specific reaction to the stressor that is provoking the imbalance; for example, the shivering and cold extremities we experience when exposed to low temperatures - both of which combine to diminish loss of heat from the body. Second, by a non-specific reaction of total internal readjustment. Dr. Hans Selye, who pioneered the medical research on stress, showed that this non-specific response calls forth the *same* biochemical, hormonal, and nervous system changes regardless the nature of the original stressor - be that physical, chemical, or emotional or, as is usual, a combination of all three. [4]

He called this *The General Adaptation Syndrome.*

It is this non-specific, internal readjustment directed toward rebalancing the body's functions and systems, and independent of the specific stressors that caused it, which is the essence of stress. We call the changes that bring about this readjustment, *The Stress Response.*

The observable and measurable signs of the Stress Response are: increased heart rate, breathing, blood pressure, metabolism and muscle blood flow. But, what happens at the functional and energy levels of the body during the stress response is very complex. There is a release of chemicals, hormones and neuro-transmitters from the brain which sets in motion further hormonal and metabolic changes. The adrenal glands release their chemicals and neurotransmitters, including adrenaline, cortisone, and related steroids, which causes active release of glycogen from the liver resulting in a rise in blood-sugar. This increase in blood-sugar, and the surge of adrenaline plus other factors readies the body for fight or flight which is the essence and purpose of the stress response. In days gone by when men and women lived closer to nature, and food had to be hunted, the fight or flight reaction was a very necessary protective mechanism. If a bear was on your tail, you would need that surge of adrenaline and blood-sugar, a fast heart rate, and rapid breathing to propel yourself up the nearest tree. But in today's society, when we are under stress, there is usually no place where we can run to. In common parlance, "All stressed up with nowhere to go!" We are caught, as it were, with all that energy and chemistry churning inside of us with no viable outlet - the reason, of course, why exercise is so good for us at any time, but particularly in times of stress. In order to sustain this reaction, the body's demands for amino acids, vitamins, elements and other nutrients increases. Add to this the de-naturation of our foods, and the need to supplement the diets of children with appropriate doses of vitamins becomes apparent.

In addition, and *central* to the ultimate fallout from stress expressed as disease or dysfunction, is its effect on the Autonomic Nervous System.

There are two major components to the nervous system:

> 1. The *Somato-Sensory*: which controls movement, sensation and speech and, so long as we remain healthy, is more or less under voluntary control; and,

> 2. The *Autonomic Nervous System*: which controls *all* other body functions.

In essence, it is the steward of every organ and system in the body. However, the Autonomic Nervous System itself responds, interplays with, and is controlled by the Hypothalamus and Limbic System and, through many other connections, interfaces and communicates with all other parts of our being and with our many layered consciousness.

The control buttons for the Autonomic Nervous System are located in the Hypothalamus which then in a sense may be regarded as a fuse box for the body's electrochemical and other messenger systems, all of which operate on memories of how to react once given a signal specific to a particular situation. These in turn are relayed to and then respond to messages from the Limbic System, the oldest part of the brain which controls emotions, and from the Cerebral Cortex where thoughts are processed. The Hypothalamus communicates with the Endocrine System through its connections with the Pituitary Gland and, through special neural connections, communicates with the entire immune system which during stress slows down its functions — T-cells diminish and have a slower rate of DNA repair, immune globulins are diminished, cortisol is increased and other interferences with normal immune functions occur.

Dr. Hans Selye described three stages of *The General Adaptation Syndrome:*

The first stage he calls the stage of "Alarm-Reaction;" the second stage he called the "Stage of Resistance" or "Adaptation;" and, the third stage he called "Exhaustion" or "Burnout."

Stage One is, for the most part, good. The alarm rings, we are warned and, if all goes well and we deal effectively with the stressors, the body re-balances itself and returns to normal. If the stress is maintained over a period of time without relief, the body begins to fail in its normal balancing process and the cascade of events that I have outlined takes on a more permanent character. The body actually adapts to the stressors and attains a level of functioning above and beyond its optimal level.

Stage Two is when *stress* becomes *distress* leading to dysfunction of the Autonomic Nervous System which impacts on all functions of the body. If unrelieved, the dysfunction can become permanent. The Hypothalamic connections I have just described, impacts on consciousness — and therefore, on thought and perception. When thought and perception become compromised, we begin to see the world through a glass, darkly. Our moods and our behavior become dysfunctional and, since we are children of God and thus spiritual beings on a human journey, therefore more than body, mind and emotion, when these are off-balance it creates a sense of disconnectedness from our spiritual core which manifests as spiritual de-vitalization.

Stage Three is when the body is overwhelmed and death ensues.

As mentioned previously, it is estimated that between 85% and 90% of all illness is stress induced. From what I have described, quite clearly the process of disease and dysfunction originates in Stage Two of the General Adaptation Syndrome or, as we also refer to it, the Stress Response.

However, the determining factor of which type of disease will ensue is genetically determined and is a function of the memories within our own unique genome.

This factor, which is at present not in the universal awareness and thus, little if ever discussed, is vital in the delicate balance that exists between health and disease of body, mind and soul. The reason for its importance is, I believe, that fundamentally it is a replay between what is within and what is without. In this case it is the tension(s) that exist at the interface where health and disease tumble and mix the two major energies: that which is within — deriving in part from our genes and in part from the memories encoded in our response systems from past experiences, and that which is without — which is our present reactions to circumstances and environment. When this combination is juxtaposed with the interchangeable nature of matter and energy, and the changeability of energy itself, it takes on profound importance in terms not only of its role in the genesis of disease but also in terms of its prevention and treatment.

Energy, and removal of obstructions to its free flow in the human body has been at the heart of Chinese Medicine for millennia. Essentially, Chinese medicine seeks to re-establish balance between the outer and the inner by re-establishing the flow of energy in organs, as well as body tissues and structures, when it has become blocked. The role of energy in Western Medicine is only at the threshold of our awareness, let alone our attention both in terms of healing, as well as causation of disease and dysfunction. Strangely, attention to it has post dated and flowed from a flood of self-help and other books published over the last 15 years or so on how to promote good health through techniques that foster balance and meaning between what is inner and what is outer. That many of these books emphasize the importance of "things" spiritual in our lives is no accident. Historically, in the West, pursuit of the nature of *unity* and *balance,* and of the connections that exist between the inner and the outer, has been the purview of theologians, philosophers, metaphysicians, mystics and other spiritual seekers. Furthermore, in our materialistic society, the spiritual has for too long been relegated to a passé dimension. Re-establishing it or putting it back where it belongs at the center of our lives serves to fill the emptiness of all else, which is a major contributing factor to the cause of stress. This of itself explains the popularity and success of these self-help books. But, as humanity matures and evolves, destiny gifts the world with some men and women of powerful intellect and deep spirituality. Their gifts to us have been and continue to be deeper insights into the unity of all things which draws back the curtains a little more on the most exquisite of all movement, the dance of the inner with the outer. Though the choreography of this dance is becoming more defined, nevertheless, the undulations of its movements remain hidden from our eyes. Its energy, however, breaks through these veils of secrecy and manifests as the dance of thought, felt emotion and behavior.

It is when the energy is negative that stress ensues.

Priest, paleontologist, and scholastic, Pierre Teilhard de Chardin, throughout his life asked, "How can the two realms of our experience, those of the outer and inner worlds be reconciled and brought to unity?"[5] The manner in which he set about addressing this problem was not primarily philosophical, the tradition from which he came, but he chose as his point of departure the methods and findings of Science. Thereafter, he sought to fit philosophical thought into his scientific hypotheses which were based on the information he had garnered from his paleontological research. As a result, he was one of the first in this century to suggest that matter — meaning particles, and energy were interchangeable. Decades later this was authenticated by Dr. David Bohm, a physicist of international renown and quantum fame, who caught on to this phenomenon and had studied it with Robert Oppenheimer, Niels Bohr and other renowned physicists.

Basing his ideas on his scientific observations of the behavior of so-called Quantum Particles, which appeared to move effortlessly from matter to energy and then from energy to matter, Dr. Bohm conceptualized matter and energy as being interchangeable and, therefore, as being one and the same thing. This led him to believe that what *is* in the Universe, and thus, within ourselves, exists within two orders: the Explicate Order — that which we can measure and more or less describe; and, the Implicate Order — that which we cannot measure and, given our present state of evolution and knowledge, cannot adequately describe. He said that there was an integral relationship between the two and, in essence, described the Explicate Order as the expression of an enfolded Implicate Order — which, due to the interchangeability of matter and energy, is in a constant state of flux. In other words, the sum of what we are at any given moment may not be the sum of what we are in subsequent moments. While this is obvious from measurable fluctuations such as those that occur with our hormones and particular body chemistries, such as glucose, on a daily basis, what is not so obvious are the fluctuations that occur in the brain and body chemistries that influence thoughts, feelings and behavior. Again, it was Pierre Teilhard de Chardin who, grasping the endless potentials inherent in the interchangeability of energy and matter, expounded at length on how the energies and memories of an observer change the nature of what is observed. Dr. Bohm and Dr. F. David Peat, amongst others, brought science to bear on the validity of this observation.[6]

Thus, in terms of managing stress and diminishing or even reversing its detrimental fallout on children and adults alike, there are two phenomena deriving from Science and the Humanities to which we need give our whole and undivided attention:

1. That energy and matter are in a constant state of movement and interchange; and,

2. That what is observed is subject to how it is observed which suggests that the observer and the observed are *one*.

Both of these phenomena directly challenge the commonly held belief that reality is an objective, rigid quantity, a rubric under which human beings are often judged and classified. Furthermore, in terms of the effects of stress and our ability to change perceptions and energies, they have profound implications for the treatment of all disease but particularly for emotional and psychiatric disorders.

Let me first address the energy that resides in the world

of the particles of matter that comprise the genes. Genes contain memories that penetrate consciousness to varying degrees. Indeed, in genetic parlance we talk about the degree of penetrance of a gene. In some cases the penetrance, i.e., its expression, is total and immutable — particularly those that determine morphology, which is what pertains to appearance, form and shape (e.g., the color of the eyes, the shape of the nose, height). In terms of disease, in some cases the memories are overwhelming in their manifestation and impact (e.g., in Huntington's Chorea, Phenyl-Ketonuria (PKU), and many others). On the other hand, there are genes with weak memories that are subject to change. Here, again, in genetic parlance, we talk about the mutation or changeability of genes. Indeed, a recent study revealed two candidate genes on chromosome #18 for Bi-Polar, Manic-Depressive Disorder.[7] The authors wisely stated that these were susceptibility genes with a complex mode of inheritance whose expression in my opinion would include and even depend on the quality of life of the individual having these genes.

I propose that the complex mode of inheritance of individuals with these and other disease susceptible, but mutable, genes relates to the degree to which their environment and experience from conception through adolescence either facilitates, diminishes or cancels their expression. I further believe that this is directly related to the number and duration of occurrences that bring about Stage Two of the *General Adaptation Syndrome*, the *Stress Response* and the degree of severity or otherwise with which Stage 2 and its fallout on body, mind and soul is experienced; particularly, whether or not there was any intervention to minimize negative effects. All of these factors directly impact on the quality of the energy that is absorbed from the world that is exterior to one's self. If we relate the facts of the interchangeability of matter and energy, and the mutability of energy itself, to the dynamics inherent in stress which is an imbalance between demands of the environment and the coping resources of the individual, we are compelled to grasp the *enormity* of what it means in assisting children to live in peace with themselves, with others and the Universe which they must share peacefully if humanity is to survive.

The enormity would mean nothing less than a radical change in how we perceive health, and no less a change in how we promote it and treat and heal its absence in disease and dysfunction. Necessary and laudable as are our efforts to ensure the physical health of children, unless we add nurturance of their souls and see this as pivotal to their emotional and physical well-being, our efforts will be so much dross across the cosmos. No idle words were they of William Blake, "If the doors of perception were cleansed, everything would appear to humankind - as it is - infinite." Both in physiological and soul terms, these words speak to the wisdom of the values that should be the heritage of every child born into the world. Alas, we have far to go. Stress on the souls of children is now their common heritage.

Notes

[1] James R. Flynn and *Scientific American*, November, 1995; Flynn, in *Psychological Bulletin*, 1984 and 1987; and *The Flynn Effect in the Bell Curve* by Charles Murray and Richard Herstein, 1995.

[2] Daniel Goleman, *Emotional Intelligence*. (Bantam Books: New York, 1995).

[3] Judith Marks Mishne, *The Learning Curve: Elevating Children's Academic & Social Comprehension*. (Jason Aronson, Inc.: New York, 1996).

[4] Hans Selye, *Stress Without Distress*. (Signet: New York, 1975).

[5] Pierre Teilhard De Chardin, *Human Energy*. (Harcourt, Brace, Jovanovich: New York; English translation, 1969, William Collins Sons & Company, LTD, London).

[6] David Bohm and F. David Peat, *Science, Order and Creativity*. (Bantam Books: London, 1987); also, F. David Peat, *Synchronistry: The Bridge Between Matter and Mind*. (Bantam Books: New York, 1987).

[7] *Chromosome 18, DNA Markers and Manic Depressive Illness*. Proceedings of the National Academy of Science, June, 1994.

V

Stress on the Souls of Children

I am the slayer of the soul
destroyer of the dream
The nightmares which recur
and wake you with your screams.

I am the end of innocence
the planting of the fear
That eats away inside your mind
and kills you year by year.

I am the words you cannot speak
the acts that you regret
The twisted childhood memories
that you cannot forget.

I am the terror in your voice
as painfully you plea
To fight the urges inside of you
to end up just like me.

Slayer of the Soul[1]

Holy Spirit,
giving life to all, moving all creatures,
root of all things, washing them clean,
wiping out their mistakes, healing their wounds.
You are our true life;
luminous, wonderful, awakening the heart
from its ancient sleep.

Hildegard of Bingen

Evening is that quiet time of day when I relish encounters with thoughts — my own and those expressed by others. One evening in early May, 1996, I was reading a review of a recently published book, *The Re-Enchantment of Everyday Life*.[2] It is the third volume in the trilogy about *soul* and *soulfull* living written by Thomas Moore. The first two in this trilogy are *Care of the Soul* and *Soul Mates*.[3] The reviewer observed that Moore had made a triumphant declaration of our need for the daily bread of spiritual nourishment! It was good that I could glow with agreement, not only because I agree and feel it deeply but it is, after all, at the center of the wisdom of all religions and eternally will be so. The reviewer went on to say that Moore had created a deeply moving and transformative vision of how we must live in order to be fully human. Yet, as my thoughts paced on I found myself grieving for the countless children and people all over the world for whom life was a daily grind for survival, let alone physical and spiritual nurturance, and whose experiences were anything but divinely human.

Then I picked up an article written by Keith Geiger, President of the National Education Association (NEA) which was published in *NEA Today*, the association's newsletter, in March of 1996.[4] In the article, Geiger recounted the story of Marcel Thornton, a Baltimore Disc Jockey. Returning home from the Million Man March on Washington, D.C. in October, 1995, Thornton vowed that he would never again broadcast popular music that degrades women and promotes sexual violence. His boss objected, and he was fired. Marcel Thornton has *no* regrets. "It became very apparent to me," he said, "that I had to take personal responsibility for what I did. As an adult, I owed it to the kids. Many adults have no idea what kids are listening to these days, - some of the stuff that is sold and put on public airways is disgusting; it encourages young men to be brutal and to degrade women."

Geiger continued,

About the same time that Thornton was fired, the advocacy group *Children Now* released the results of a poll that provided chilling corroboration of his cause. Forty percent of girls 14-17 said either they or a friend their own age had been hit or beaten by a boyfriend.

Juliet assaulted by Romeo?

Other polls have shown that a shockingly large percentage of girls and young women growing up in America today have been, as a U.S. Department of Education report states, 'subjected to a pattern of overt sexual hostility accompanied by actual or threatened physical contact and the repeated use of obscene or foul language.'

Unfortunately, headlines like 'Sexual Harassment Makes School Hellish for Girls,' seen recently in the *St. Louis Post-Dispatch*, aren't all that uncommon.

For educators, the evidence is overwhelming: Sexual abuse and harassment can stunt the intellectual and emotional development of girls and young women.

It's high time that men of all ages in our society started standing up, as Marcel Thornton did, to the sexual bullies and those in the entertainment business (music, video games and television) who egg them on.

We have a long way to go. Too many adults have been moral spectators for too long. How else could we have sunk to the intolerable situation girls and young women find themselves in today?

We need to heed the recent words of Children's Defense Fund leader Marian Wright Edelman when she says: "I worry with every fiber of my being about our many children who, lacking a sense of the sacred or internal moral moorings, are trying to grow up in a society without boundaries, without respect.

"Never have we exposed children so early and relentlessly to cultural messages glamorizing violence, sex, possessions, alcohol and tobacco, with so few mediating influences from responsible adults."[5]

Sufficient as all of this was for a period of inner withdrawal for prayer and meditation for a world deprived of spiritual nurturance, nevertheless, I continued on through the pile of literature still awaiting my attention. *"GOVERNMENT CONDEMNED FOR JEOPARDIZING CHILDREN"* boomed the headline on the front page of the May, 1996 issue of the American Academy of Pediatrics News. At the Spring session of the Academy held in Chicago in April, 1996, it's President, Dr. Ed Keenan declared that the policies of the United States of America have successfully pushed children into poverty. Stating that "the lives of children are too precious to gamble with their future," he said "they have become a bureaucratic afterthought."[6] Could this really be true of the wealthiest nation in the world? And, if there is no concern for their physical well-being, what does it tell us about the lack of concern for their spiritual nurturance? Sadly, all too much.

In his keynote address to the same gathering of Academy members, Bob Greene, a columnist with the *Chicago Tribune*, implored Pediatricians to use their influence and clout to preserve children's rights and dignity. For several years Greene has devoted most of his newspaper column to heightening the awareness of his readers to the plight of abused and neglected children. He said,

> 'To me, the worst enemies children have are not drugs or street gangs, but those government and judicial groups that fail children,' Green said. 'You can arrest a drug dealer or a gang member, but when the highest court in a state fails a child, there's no recourse.'
>
> Many people don't want to hear the terrible crimes committed against children, he conceded, but the stories must be told to help other children.
>
> 'We can't keep our mouths shut,' Greene said. 'We can't be silent.'
>
> Greene recounted the cases of several Illinois children placed in harm's way because the state judicial system failed to determine the types of environments into which it was thrusting young people.

In a case involving a child Greene called 'Sarah,' the girl was born to a drug addicted prostitute and abandoned two days after her birth. When 'Sarah' was 5, a judge ruled that the mother was reformed. The girl's adopted parents were ordered to give the child to the natural mother and her boyfriend.

The natural mother tore up pictures the girl had of her adopted family and hid the child's scrapbook, Greene said.

He also cited the 'Baby Richard' case, which received national attention a year ago when the Illinois Supreme Court ruled that the adopted boy had to be returned to his natural parents.

'I've never encountered that kind of *meanness* in a court,' Greene said, as he recalled the day the natural parents arrived at the adopted parents' home to take the child last April.

The columnist, who witnessed the incident in the home that day, heard Richard sobbing: 'Please don't make me go. I'll be good.'

'How do you explain to a 4-year-old child that someone he's never met is going to drive him away in a half-hour?' Greene said. 'I wish those five judges would have had the guts to face that child that day.'

...A more recent case tugging at Greene's heart, and one to which he planned to devote several columns, involves an 8-year-old boy, 'Joe.'

The child currently faces aggravated criminal sexual assault charges – felony charges if committed by an adult.

When the boy was 2, an appellate court ruled that a couple, selected by Lutheran Social Services of Illinois to adopt the child, could no longer care for the child.

The boy's biological mother didn't want the child back herself. Instead, she asked two friends – a convicted felon and his girlfriend – to care for her son.

After the couple broke up, the woman and Joe later moved in with a man who had been in prison for criminal sexual assault.

By the time Joe had reached first grade, he had been in six different schools and was ruled by school officials to be suicidal and a danger to himself or others.

'An 8-year-old, his life shattered, has to face a court,' Greene said. 'This child had a wonderful home and the court did this to him. Something terrible happened. It was the responsibility of the court to see where the boy was going.[7]

Speaking for myself, I have long been dismayed at the repetitive victimization endured by neglected and abused children as well as by many other children. In the USA, as in many Western countries, their future is decided *not* by those having knowledge and expertise in child development but ultimately by the judicial system. Judges with little or no such knowledge are called upon to make these decisions. All too frequently children are placed in situations so detrimental to their emotional and soul well-being, their consequent feelings of hopelessness, loneliness, disconnectedness and rage leads them into dysfunctional and often violent behavior. The pervasiveness of these tragedies was highlighted in the following editorial from London's *The Independent:*

> A national scandal is unfolding in North Wales: a report into what could be Britain's most appalling child abuse case is being suppressed. The scandal is not just that at least 100, and possibly double that number, children were systematically abused, while in the 'care' of the state in the 1970s and Eighties. It is that a 300 page report into the affair has not been published and there is little sign that it will be soon.
>
> The scandal is one of the most organized and widespread cases of child abuse yet discovered, involving a network of people in different local authority homes. At least 16 former inmates of the homes have since died, several through suicide, in circumstances that were related to their dreadful treatment. It is not as if the authorities were unaware of what has gone on. Since 1974, more than 50 staff have been disciplined and several have been convicted. Yet none of the 14 reports into the affair, 12 of them internal, has been published. This is a cover-up on a massive scale. The public is being denied information about how services operated in its name have been systematically exploited for the purposes of sexual abuse of the most

vulnerable children. Victims are being denied access to the information they need for redress.[8]

Though it is rarely if ever a topic for discussion, let alone of scholarly or psychological inquiry, the fact is that all countries in the technologically developed world have a heavy history of using and abusing children in the sweat shops of labor upon which hegemonies, empires and monetary wealth have been based and built. Believed to have started during the Industrial Revolution, this abuse actually predated that era by many centuries; a topic which I have addressed in another forthcoming book.[9] In this period of human history the use and abuse of children, and the overflow of what historically has been considered their usability and dispensability, is finding its mark through their sexual and pornographic exploitation; the bottom line of which remains as before, profits for their elders. But, this is not all. The issues of child labor in manufacturing and mining industries, as well as in agriculture and forced and bonded labor, has recently gained the attention of the International community. With input from countless individuals and organizations all over the world, the staff of the International Child Labor Study Group of the United States Bureau of International Labor Affairs published in two volumes in 1995 and 1996 comprehensive reports which define worldwide abuse of children.[10] Furthermore, the rapidly increasing numbers of children requiring foster, residential and other protective services in the Western world, as well as the inadequacy of resources to meet their needs, has been described as nothing less than a national emergency.[11] It is clear that the abusive use of children is being fostered not only in the Western nations but throughout the world. Mention has already been made of their role in physical combat and war.

Whether enlisted as soldiers or not, wars that ensue from historical, ethnic, religious and racial animosities end up hurting children not only physically, but in their souls — the core of their beings wherein should reside the feeling of the security of love and from which compassion for others should flow. It is well documented that children who witness violence can be as traumatized as those who are victims of it.[12] Likewise, embargoes on regimes for whatever seemingly good reasons end up hurting them.

All this brings to focus a curious paradox. First, within all the rhetoric we are hearing from all sectors of society on both sides of the Atlantic and beyond, about the need to *return* to basic values, there must be at its core not only a voiceless general agreement that there is a commonly shared energy to which we must *return,* but also a deeply felt longing for its presence in our midst.

What by any other name is this energy
if not of God!

If this be so, then by using and abusing children are we not abusing the very energy by which they and we can be spiritually nurtured. Likewise, by injuring and negatively altering the energies that connect the souls of children to their source in creative love, God, we are ignoring and at best sidelining the power through which "all things are made new." And because memory is the vehicle of life and the infrastructure upon which our perceptions, thoughts, feelings and, thus, our behaviors are built, the felt absence of spiritual nurturance during infancy and childhood persists into adolescence and adulthood. Thus, if there is no intervention, we are also abbreviating, if not blocking, their ability to seek this nurturance for themselves as their lives unfold. Meanwhile, too often these young people are blamed for the dilemmas of society.

When I graduated from Medical School so many years ago, it seems now like it was in another lifetime, my mother's gift to me was a very unusual cameo brooch that I still treasure. Rather than the customary beauty of a woman's face engraved on the tortoise shell, it shows Christ Jesus blessing children. She knew of my desire to become a Pediatrician, and, so, in the note that accompanied it, she said:

"May your love for children and your service to them mirror the love that Christ Jesus had for them; and when your human journey is done, may you and the world know that you faithfully responded to his call. 'Suffer the children to come unto me for of such is the Kingdom of God'."

While I pray that the pure, empathic and unconditional love of which my mother spoke may continue to my dying day, I have also in my long journey been made terribly aware of why Christ Jesus added an admonition. "Should anyone hurt one of these innocents," he said, "it would be better that a mill stone be hung around his neck and then that they be flung into the sea."

The reverence for children to which Jesus called us was no idle invitation. In essence, because the feelings, behavior and belief systems of our adult life are moulded from the memories of our beginning and our childhood, it speaks to the quality of energy through which individuals and humanity exercises *power*, an energy that emanates from memories within the soul. When this energy is violated or in anyway stressed, it causes trauma to the soul of the individual — which in aggregate speaks to the trauma of society, and it is this trauma which causes divisions between individuals and nations.

Trauma to the soul is always the result of the denigration or violation of the trinity of personhood — body, mind and soul. It can be inflicted by word, deed or both — or even by the conveyance of the negative energy of thought and look, all or any of which can result in a loss of self identity. Furthermore, regardless the source, and by whatever means the injury is inflicted, a part of one's own identity is projected onto those who cause the injury, which eventually becomes emotional bondage to an-other. Thus, children, dependent as they are upon the adults in their lives for a sense of belonging and nurturance, will not uncommonly choose to be with an abusing parent or surrogate rather than in a safe place. Given the fact that the soul expresses itself through feelings, the reason is apparent. If the primal feelings of connection to Creation become submerged by all that serves to disconnect it from this source, and thus, from its true identity, it will inevitably reach for expression through that which it has come to know and experience as its connection. Thus, if feelings deriving from abuse, betrayal or torture become its predominant connections to Life, these then become the memories in the soul. Residing within these memories are the energies that prompt perception and personal behavior. When encoded in the genes it promotes trans-generational transference.

It is my belief that *soul trauma* is at the root of all psychiatric disorders. If one carefully evaluates the symptoms of these afflictions one can see in them the fallout of their origins in fear, anxiety, abandonment, sadness, confusion and rage which always ensue from injury to the soul, all of which serve to disconnect self from one's own unique identity. These and other emotions are powerful stressors that call forth the Stress Response, whose legacies as already described are dysfunction of mind, body and soul.

For too long we have attributed the measurable changes

in chemistry and function that accompany most if not all psychiatric disorders as their cause. I believe the contrary is the case; that they are the consequences of the changes in body and brain chemistry that result from the stressors that cause injury to e-motion (that is, energy-in-motion) and soul. The latest psychiatric code book used by mental health professionals, the *Diagnostic and Statistical Manual of Psychiatric Disorders* (DSM-IV), published in 1994 by the American Psychiatric Association, contains a new category for disturbances of a spiritual or religious nature. Many practitioners of transpersonal psychology hailed this development for it enables them to *officially* recognize and treat, without being thought odd by their colleagues, many situations they had been regularly encountering. While this is a great leap out of the concrete of the former rather mechanical and analytical approach to the cause of psychiatric disorder, we still have far to go before we fully recognize the power of the energy of the soul and how it drives changes in brain and body chemistry, and not the other way around.

In general, it can be said that there are three stages of reaction to soul trauma, which are identifiable from early infancy onwards. In the first stage, there is confusion hence, several competing emotions struggle for expression. Basically, it is a reaction of grief at the trashing or invasion of personhood or its neglect and abandonment. The resulting sense of powerlessness and helplessness lead to denial, sadness, anger and even blind rage. In infants and young children this leads to the syndrome called, "Failure to Thrive." The child withdraws from its unloving and often hostile environment, refuses to eat, shrinks from touch and, if there is no intervention, will die. During and following World War II, many infants and children were orphaned and put in orphanages where they were simply warehoused. Death from the absence of love was a frequent occurrence.[13] In recent years, events and wars all over the world have inflicted similar horrors on these innocents to the tune of the death of millions of them. Those who survive the early onset of soul trauma invariably exhibit in later childhood signs of RADIEC, whose symptoms, described in footnote #4 of *Chapter 2*, act like tentacles squeezing and inhibiting the energies within the soul. The suffering of these children, those who survive as well as those who don't, cry to the world for the nurturance of the sacredness of their beings.

The second stage of soul trauma is a period of transition wherein the emotional effects of the trauma become grafted on to the personality of the individual. It can last from several months to a year or more depending upon the age of onset and how well immunized the soul was prior to the attack on its integrity. By this I mean how well ingrained are the memories of connectedness to love and creation. This, of course, depends on the quality of the energy at the beginning of life as well as on the energy in the genes and the environment within which the child subsequently existed. The more positive these energies the greater will be the resilience and, therefore, the resistance to permanent dysfunction. This is why the energy of the parents during and following conception is so vital to the well-being of their children about which more will be said later. But, for children who have endured the early onset of soul trauma, the dysfunctional behaviors classified as adjustment disorders of emotion and behavior which characterize this second stage and which appear from about the age of two on upwards — combined with the long-term sequence of RADIEC — takes on more ominous long-term prognoses than those who have not.

The third stage is one of consolidation. The trauma takes

up a felt residence in the soul whose message is that all that is external to personhood is hostile and to be feared. This fear expresses its disconnection from the source of love and creation in serious psychiatric disorders and in violence inflicted upon others, and often upon self. These psychiatric disorders are classified in the DSM IV according to their symptomatology but they all derive from the same source — soul trauma — whether the symptoms fall into the category of affective disorders, the many so-called personality disorders, and the many dissociative disorders such as Schizophrenia, Multiple Personality, Manic-Depressive disorders and others.

The type of disorder is determined genetically. This means that at some point in the lives of our familial ancestors, they reacted to soul stress in a way that stressed the capacity of particular genes that control emotions and behavior to maintain balance and function. If these weakened genes and their altered energy find no surcease from their fragility in succeeding generations or are assaulted by further trauma, they will continue to manifest as soul dysfunction and psychiatric disorder, all depending on a critical level of environmental stress that will release their dysfunctional energy in Stage Two of the General Adaptation Syndrome in those who carry them.

It is, I believe, altered energy and its altered messages that initiate and then maintain the electrochemical changes in body, mind and brain which, being measurable up until now, we have believed to be the cause of psychiatric disorder. If this is so, the implications for treatment and healing take on a unprecedented aura of light and hope. For by changing the quality of the energy, we change the quality of life's experience

Thus, it is clear that to inflict trauma on the soul, whether it be one's own soul or that of another — worst of all a child's soul, is to darken the light of love and weaken the bonds of connectedness to our source in God. To be separated from our source by whatever means is surely a property and dimension of *evil*. The Christian Scriptures teach us to call good and evil by name, but it also teaches, "Do not be conquered by evil but conquer evil with good."[14] In his book, *Crossing the Threshold Of Hope*, Pope John Paul II stated that, "...therein Christian morality is expressed. If this morality strives toward values, if it brings a universal affirmation of good, it can be nothing but extraordinarily demanding; it is always the 'hard road' of which Christ speaks. Therefore the joy of good and the hope of its triumph in man and in the world do not exclude fear for this good, for the disappearance of this hope. And it is precisely from this struggle for the victory of good in man and in the world that the need for prayer arises"[15]

Surely these statements apply most directly to children.

There can be no doubt that humanity is presently emerging from the dark age of mechanistic technology and a belief that science can answer all questions and meet all needs. As a reaction to how these beliefs have starved the soul of humanity, we have in recent years been satiated with a plethora of books and television programs whose messages have undeniably addressed our spiritual essence and the need for prayer at all times and in all of our lives. At the center of all that can be said and has been written about prayer, *prayer* remains simply and powerfully the raising up, the giving over, of our hearts, minds and soul to God. It is such a simple concept. Yet, as the concert pianist makes the most difficult piece of music flow with ease after years of discipline and practice, so it is with prayer; "Seek ye first the Kingdom of God and all things will be added to you."[16] Seeking requires a daily practice, a daily discipline and a call to faith when the journey seems dry, hard and lacking in any sense of comfort. The ultimate prayer of yielding ourselves to the Infinite often begins with the prayers of request and intercession which is frequently accompanied with bargaining. So, when we speak of prayer it is often within this latter context. Yet, however much we reach for the prayer of yielding our lives to the kingdom, and however fervent we are, we live in the world. Therefore, exigencies of the moment often conflict with our good intentions and end up directing our actions. The Second Vatican Council's *Pastoral Constitution On the Modern World (Gaudium et Spes)* addresses this very issue.

> The truth is that the imbalances under which the modern world labors are linked with that more basic imbalance rooted in the heart of man. For in man himself many elements wrestle with one another. Thus, on the one hand, as a creature he experiences his limitations in a multitude of ways. One the other, he feels himself to be boundless in his desires and summoned to a higher life.
>
> Pulled by manifold attractions, he is constantly forced to choose among them and to renounce some. Indeed, as a weak and sinful being, he often does what he would not, and fails to do what he would. Hence he suffers from internal divisions, and from those flow so many and such great discords in society.
>
> Nevertheless, in the face of the modern development of the world, an ever-increasing number of people are raising the most basic questions or recognizing them with a new sharpness: what is man? What is this sense of sorrow, of evil, of death, which continues to exist despite so much progress? What is the purpose of these victories, purchased at so high a cost? What can man offer to society, what can he expect from it? What follows this earthly life?[17]

Commenting on this passage, Pope John Paul II observed that "questioning God's existence is intimately united with the purpose of human existence. Not only is it a question of intellect; it is also a question of the will, even a question of the human heart." And, while unquestionably a part of the journey, shouldn't the prayer that seeks the Kingdom of God within be its constant companion?

For a nation whose motto is, "In God We Trust," the United States of America seems bent on side-lining God from the lives of children. Prayer in school has been abolished on the grounds that it conflicts with the United States Constitution that requires separation of Church and State. Surely this is to ignore that though there are many religions, there is only one God. Banishing God on constitutional or political grounds in the environment, where they spend a large part of their growing years, is to deny children the memories that God was a part of it. Just the simple mention of God, repeated daily like a mantra during their formative years, embeds in their psyche memories and energies that could serve them well in many situations throughout their journeys. The call to God and spiritual nurturance resides within every moment and every occurrence of our life. This being so, then the promise of our connection to God lies not in some distant future and yet-to-be-experienced paradise but, right now and right here, within our human journey.

Who is teaching children this reverence for the uniqueness and opportunities of their human journeys and that of others? Given the statistics, it is safe to assume that this is rarely a part of their learning. So when a child or young adult tells you that there is no God, and that Love does not exist, do not respond by disclaiming the values of these young people; rather, look to the legacies they have inherited that make them so.

Notes

[1] This poem was written by a child molester. Taken from Stephen J. Rosetti's *Slayer of the Soul: Child Sexual Abuse and the Catholic Church*. Second Printing. (Twenty-Third Publications: Mystic, CT) 1990, 1991.

[2] Thomas Moore, *Re-Enchantment of Everyday Life*. (HarperCollins: New York, 1996).

[3] Thomas Moore, *Care of the Soul: A Guide To Cultivating Depth and Sacredness In Everyday Life*. (HarperCollins: New York, 1992); and, *Soul Mate* (HarperCollins, New York, 1994).

[4] Keith Geiger, in *NEA Today* (March, 1996).

[5] Gerry Clark, "Government Condemned For Jeopardizing Children," *AAP News* 12, 5 (May, 1996):1.

[6] Ibid.

[7] Ibid., p.8.

[8] Taken from an editorial in *The Independent*, (Saturday, 13 April 1996), London, England.

[9] Yet to be published, *Immunology of the Soul: Understanding and Healing the Scars On the Souls of Children*.

[10] Two volume print set.

[11] Richard D. Krugman, "The Disintegrating Child Protection System," *Pediatric News* (January, 1996).

[12] L. Terr, "What Happens To Early Memories of Trauma." *Journal of the American Academy of Child & Adolescent Psychiatry*. 27 (1988):96-104; also, E.M. Cummings, D. Vogel, et. al. "Children's Responses To Different Forms Of Expressing Anger Between Adults," *Child Development* 52 (1989):1274-1282.

[13] John Bowlby, *Child Care And the Growth Of Love*. Abridged and edited by Margery Fry (1953). Based on permission of the World Health Organization on the report *Maternal Care and Mental Health*.

[14] Romans 12:21.

[15] His Holiness, Pope John Paul II, *Crossing The Threshold of Hope*. (Knopf: New York, 1994); and Matthew 7:14.

[16] Matthew 6:33.

[17] Walter M. Abbott, *The Documents of Vatican II*. "The Pastoral Constitution On the Church In the Modern World" *(Gaudium et Spes)*. (Herder and Herder: New York, 1966): Article 10.

VI

The Promise of Life
Is the Journey

I shall put my Spirit in you and you will live.

Ezekiel 17:12

Oh, the fabulous wings unused,
folded in the heart.

"A Sleep of Prisoners"
Christopher Fry

If we take the worlds enduring religions at
their best,
we discover the distilled wisdom of the human
race.

The Wisdom of Faith
Houston Smith

All creation has its origins and its life in Divine Energy.

Manifested in an infinite variety of wave patterns, many of which no doubt still remain to be discovered, they intersect eternally to render the forms and functions we perceive as reality. In the microcosm of these energies are the human form and function, identifiable as I and Thou to each of which there is a basic rhythm, a wave pattern of upswings and downslopes that is the journey of each individual life.

It is a universal axiom that we humans tend to concentrate on the downsides of our life experiences. And it is the cascade of negative energies let loose by our attachment to the downside which separates us from the creative and loving source of our beings. Our sense of loss and separation when the "bad" things happen is actually grief in action. No wonder then that all manner of books, tapes and television programs on how to be upbeat and in-touch with ourselves, with others, and the world find such a wide and hungry audience. Christ Jesus said:

"I came that you might have *Life* and have it more abundantly."[1]

"I am the *way*, the *truth* and the *life*."[2]

After feeding the five thousand with the loaves and fishes, Jesus, said,

"These things and even greater shall you do if you believe for I go to my father in heaven."[3]

And yet, like the child who is separated from its mother at

birth, we think, we feel and we behave as though we are irretrievably separated from the source and nurturance of our beings. Following the example of the man who, having found the pearl of great price, and buried it, we likewise bury these pearls of sublime promises under the sometimes unbearable weight of our negative trans-generational memories and personal experience. Alas, too often these inform us that the promises could be a meaningless sham. But, wasn't the life and journey of Christ Jesus himself, who said he came that we might have Life, full of darkness, as well as light; betrayal, as well as fidelity; hate, as well as love; despair, as well as hope?

"Father, if you are willing, take this cup away from me; still, not my will but yours be done."[4] In this one eloquent prayer, Jesus gave his *fiat* to the meaning of his life not only at that moment of almost unbearable suffering, but for eternity and, in so doing, embraced the contradictions that made his life *whole* and his mission complete.

The contradiction is timeless.

The struggle to make sense of it is the message at the core of all religions. The ability to make of all of our experiences a hymn of growth into connection with our source is the *Promise* of the journey we call *Life*. The *End* is the connection that we yearn for beyond all that distracts us; always teasingly out of our reach yet, within it; the unattainable end toward which we are bidden to strive.

In our journey to find this hidden treasure we often fail to see the paths that can lead us to it, even though they are right in front of us. Like Mary of Magdala who on the first Easter morning, went to the tomb where her Rabbouni had been laid to rest, to minister to him in death as she had done so often during his life. An angel greeted her and said, *"Woman, why are you weeping?'* She said to him, *'They have taken my*

Lord and I don't know where they laid him.' When she had said this, she turned around and saw Jesus there, but did not know it was Jesus. Jesus said to her, *'Woman, why are you weeping? Whom are you looking for?'* She thought it was the gardener and said to him, *'Sir, if you carried him away, tell me where you laid him, and I will take him.'* Jesus said to her, *'Mary!'*. She turned and said to him, *Rabbouni'*."[5] Like Mary, the beliefs and values that life and living have imprinted on our emotions and behavioral responses blind us to the possibilities that exist beyond them. That her Rabbouni would rise from the dead was as foreign to the beliefs of Mary of Magdala as is the possibility that the dysfunction and violence that pervades our society and the world can find its healing. In the very instant wherein she recognized him, she knew that, contrary to her belief that he was dead, Christ Jesus was alive forever as the bearer and giver of the pearl of great price — the connection to life divine.

Most of the human race has for millennia gone its way of deafness to the real message of *life* and *living*. The promise and the end have yielded to a reality so far distant from them that in the United States of America the telephone connection to Emergency services, the famous "911" number, is no longer able to cope with the demands.[6] In 1995, in Miami, Florida alone, 1.2 million calls were made for help, often prompted by violence. The system is so overloaded that many victims get recorded messages that tell them to call back.

Was the life and message of Jesus an aberration in the history of humankind?

Was the Christ Jesus event a sweet interlude whose true meaning went to heaven along with its messenger?

Hardly!

Across all cultures and religions, and throughout recorded history, there have been many who stopped to listen and respond to the quiet beyond the noise and the light beyond the darkness — the rhythms of their lives. Some have returned from their encounters with life's precious message as did Mary of Magdala and have gifted us with their insights and words. Their message is that life derives from a common source which is divine, and that the central purpose of our lives is to open our hearts to the divine presence; to know it and love it as the essence of whom we are; to feel it and exalt in it within ourselves, as well as to respect it in others. These messages are often thought to be the territory of mystics, spiritual gurus and, yes, even religious fanatics. For most people these messages are merely interesting stories that have no relevance for them in their life. But such, in fact, is not the case. The urge to know and feel love is a shared inheritance of all of humankind. It is when this inheritance is stolen that the resulting sense of separation leads to confusion, despair, jealousy, hatred and violence.

Indeed, such are the messages of the scriptures that all religions give to us.

In the Hebrew scriptures, once banished from their constant awareness of their source in love and creation, Adam by his words was the first to point fingers of blame for his dispossession at Eve, his female companion; a scenario, alas, that persists even today! And their children, carrying the memory of the dispossession of their parents, visited their anguish on each other and every succeeding generation. Thus began in the Judeo-Christian tradition the conflict and the struggle between good and evil, light and dark, which legacy resides within every human soul.

In Hinduism, this legacy is addressed in the Bhagavad Gita which has been the exemplary text of Hinduism for millennia. Hinduism is not based on the teachings of a founder such as Buddha, Christ and Mohammed. Rather, it has emerged as a religion through the interplay of diverse beliefs and practices of the many cultures of the Indian subcontinent. It's basic concept — in Sanskrit, Dharma — means "sacred duty". This refers to the moral order that is necessary to sustain the cosmos, society and the individual and conveys a deep awareness of their interdependence. The Sanskrit title, Bhagavad Gita, has usually been interpreted to mean "Song of the Lord". However, it is actually a philosophical poem composed in the form of a dialogue between the warrior, Arjuna, the individual, his family society and his charioteer, the God, Krishna, who represents the Cosmos. It tells of the paralyzing conflict Arjuna endures when faced with a choice between good and evil, as well as the meaning of life itself. To fully understand it, one must put it into context.

The religious and cultural life of the Indian subcontinent, and much of the rest of Asia, has been deeply influenced by the Mahabharata, as well as by the Ramayana – two ancient Indian epics, which to the Western mind might be regarded as scripture. Both poems have their roots in legendary events which took place in the period following the entry of nomadic Indo-Aryan speaking tribes into northwestern India in 1200 BC. The central issue that is addressed is the war between good and evil. The setting of the Gita is the battlefield of Kurukshetra. This is not only a physical place, but it is representative of a state of mind and the desires of the soul. The essence and the message of dialogue between Arjuna and Krishna is the dilemma of Arjuna at the circumstances in which he finds himself which results from Krishna's command that Arjuna kill his enemies who are, in fact, his kinsmen. To Arjuna, Krishna is a companion and a teacher, as well as the

God who commands devotion. He is, therefore, perceived by Arjuna as the essence of all good. Therefore, when Krishna instructed him to kill those who are close to him, Arjuna feels confused and desolate at the factors in his life beyond his control that make him an unwilling player in the drama of evil versus good. But as the story of the battlefield and the inner-contest and conflict continue, Arjuna's confidence and faith increase. As he gradually lets go of his own limited vision of the cosmos, he journeys into Krishna's revelation of its awesome dimensions and then perceives the necessity of accepting his own part in it, no matter what the circumstances may be. In this manner, Arjuna is similar to Christ who was called upon to sacrifice his own life, not because of his unworthiness but for the greater good of humankind. Arjuna sees that Krishna throughout the battle was in fact addressing his (Arjuna's) emotional and earthly attachments, uncertainties and inability to act. And in the process of his acceptance of his role, Arjuna enlarges his awareness of the meaning of his conflicts and his journey which lie beyond his own personal and social values. Thus, eventually, he comes to see himself as a part of the divine plan which is reflective of divinity itself. The cry of Jesus, "Father, let this cup pass from me," is just one of the many corollaries that exist between the Bhavagad Gita and the Christian scriptures.[7] Father Bede Griffiths, O.S.B., an English-born Benedictine Monk who lived in India for thirty years, wrote a Christian commentary on the Bhavagad Gita which he aptly titled *The River Of Compassion*.[8] In the forward of his book, Fr. Bede observed that "a Christian who is open to the message of the Gita will find that it throws new light on many aspects of the gospel, and at the same time, how the Bhavagad Gita gathers a new meaning when seen in the perspective of the gospel."

Father Bede, who died in 1993, was one of those great souls who, while being thoroughly faithful to his own Christian tradition, believed that as all peoples share a common humanity, so, also, must they share the insights and gifts of all the different religious traditions of the world. A dream, perhaps, but if it were a dream come true, it would signal the end of divisions and of wars.

Next to the Bhavagad Gita the Tao of Chinese Confucianism is the most translated book in the world. The Tao, which means *way*, is at the heart of the Tao Te Ching, which is the centerpiece of all Chinese religion and thought. By subscribing to the notion that there is an over-arching *way* that encompasses everything in the universe, it resonates with other major religious scriptures the world over. While Tao means the *way*, Te conveys *a way of integrity* — meaning the totality of an individual, including his or her moral stance whether it be good or bad. Ching is the standard Chinese term for scripture. However, its basic meaning is "the warp of a fabric." And from this is derived the idea of "passing through", "experiencing", and "transacting". In the translation of Buddhist texts into Chinese use, Ching is the equivalent of the Sanskrit word Sutra, which means thread. When compared with the English word suture, Sutra applies to the stitching that holds a manuscript together, as well, indeed, it means in present medical parlance the stitches that reconnect severed human tissue; to which may be added, the fabric of the human soul. Within the context of the religious and philosophical text, *Tao* is the all-pervading, self-existent, eternal, cosmic unity -- the source from which all created things emanate and to which they will return.

This description could equally serve for the meaning of Brahman, the central principle in Indian philosophy and religion, as the energy which exists within all living things. Brahman, like the Tao, is unborn and birthless. This relates to the second person of the Christian Trinity of father, son and spirit; wherein Jesus, who emanated from the father, brought the spirit with him and was the son of the eternal, timeless, unborn God of the Judeo-Christian tradition. Jesus was the messenger who brought the script of how humans should live their lives. Entering fully into his mission, he endured all that continues to confuse our living. His reactions to the situations that threatened or upheld him are the guideposts for our reactions to similar situations within our lives. He never denied the reality of hatred and violence, but gave us his example of how we are to react to them. During the final insult to his goodness, when he was crucified as a common criminal, he asked forgiveness of eternal energy for those who persecuted him. "I thirst," he said while hanging on the cross, in reference not only to his physical thirst but for future generations who would not hear his message nor follow his example. He showed us also that out of destruction flows creation: they are not different, nor are they enemies; they are part of the same fabric and, together, make a whole; the sutra that holds all together. Harmony is the meeting place of their polarities. Christ certainly felt the tug between his public life of service — with all of its accompanying snipeings and criticisms deriving from the jealousies of others — and the life that nourished him through his *oneness* with the Father. But he also gave us the paradigm for bringing about harmony between the two. Removing himself from the arena and tumults of life as he so often did in order to be alone to pray and reconnect in stillness to the *oneness* with eternal energy in the Father, he showed us how necessary it was for us to do likewise. And as a metaphor of sorts, we who make ourselves so busy about transient things, need to retreat from them in silence and be still so that in the space between the two, we will touch and feel and know that same eternal energy.

These appositional forces are a universal human experience. Indeed, life itself, as the epigrams of the Tao Te Ching declare, is full of contradictions:

> "The bright way seems dim,
> the forward way seems backward,
> the level way seems bumpy...."

And, in addressing these contradictions, the several paths of Buddhism exhort us to detachment from all that is external to us. Giving our energy and attention to external factors is to give away the energy within our soul to things that don't nourish us, thus dimming enlightenment and obstructing the flow of divine and life-giving energy within us. Thus does Buddhism teach the wisdom of savoring the moment and of being mindful that, regardless the nature of its experience, it is a part of the *whole*.

Thus, the message and the promise inherent in all religions is that life is a journey of contrasts; that by accepting the apparent contradictions in our life we can through prayer and stillness find harmony and balance within the space where their polarities meet and from out of which we are nourished with Eternal Energy. Thus do we enter into the continuing work of Creation which ultimately is a work of *Love*. Pope John Paul II has said,

> The Gospel declares above all else the joy of creation. Creation was given and entrusted to humankind as a duty representing not a source of suffering but the foundation of a creative existence in the world. A person who believes in the essential goodness of all creation is capable of

disovering all the secrets of creation in order to perfect the work assigned to him by God — continually."[9]

That this is true, is the gift to all of humankind of the life of President Nelson Mandela of South Africa. Imprisoned for 27 years because he believed in the divine dignity of God within all creation - regardless of race, religion or creed — he maintained within his heart a belief in the inherent goodness of all humanity. In his autobiography, *Long Walk To Freedom*, he says, "Even in the grimmest times in prison when my comrades and I were pushed to our limits, I would see a glimmer of humanity in one of the guards, perhaps for just a second, but it was enough to reassure me and keep me going. Man's goodness is a flame that can be hidden but never extinguished."[10] If ever a man entered fully — and continually — into the work assigned to him by God, it was President Mandela. His years of imprisonment fully acquainted him with every conceivable human deprivation and indignity; his soul was seared by the harassment and sufferings endured by his wife and family. Likewise, during his incarceration, his oldest son, Nadiba Thembekile, was killed in a car crash and his mother died. "I do not have words to express the sorrow or the loss I felt," he said. Yet, this same man brought about the greatest, and certainly the fastest change in human relations and politics that has ever occurred, truly a great work of creation. His example is a far cry from the commonly held belief in Western cultures that there should be no pain in our lives — that there should be no dimness when there could be brightness, no backwardness when we seem set on a course of forwardness, and that our journey should be level and not bumpy.

In my many encounters with children, they have often told me, *"I deserve more."* When I ask, "What is more?", they invariably respond, *"more things."* When I ask about love, many respond by telling me that it does not exist. And yet, when I press them on, they tell me that "things" would give them a sense of belonging to others from whom they feel disconnected. Of course, what they are telling me is that they feel disconnected from the source of their life which is love and creation, and that the memories within their souls deny them the resilience they need to healthfully encounter and grow through the dim and bumpy ways.

Lest the reader think that I am a scholar removed from the experience of life, let me reassure you that life has come to me in all of its abundance. In many colors it has rendered to me the full spectrum of its energies that now are merging into the *oneness* of the rainbow from which they came. In my growing years in England during World War II, separation from home and family was a norm for children of my generation. All over Europe, indiscriminate bombings took place for a period of several years almost on a nightly basis. Many of us were sent to the countryside. I was sent to a Boarding school in Wales. The uncertainties of the war years, combined with the God and prayer-centered life I lived as a convent school girl, served to reinforce the qualities of resilience already deeply rooted in my soul as, indeed, they are rooted in the soul of every living human being just awaiting their expression. Not only through my growing years but throughout my life, I somehow have known that the obstacles to my personal oneness with creation and love were gifts in disguise to my becoming to them. Thus, in my young womanhood, I was attracted to the works and thoughts of Père Pierre Teilhard de Chardin, Teresa of Avila, Thomas Merton, Mary Ward, Meister Eckhart and countless others of this and other generations and cultures who were brave enough to share their journeys with the rest of the world. Yet, as I matured, I realized that whatever they had to say — marvelous as it was — became simply guideposts to my own journey of becoming. One cannot know *oneness* through another. Each one of us has to grow and mature into co-inherence with our source and our being, and our life within it. Organized religion and the thoughts of others can certainly help us on our way, but the journey toward what appears to be the yet unattainable end must always be traveled one at a time no matter the throng of companions. And this is what children need to know in their hearts and feel within their souls; all children, those that have been condemned to sweat and toil; those materially better-off but spiritually starved through neglect, abuse and abandonment; the privileged and all the in-betweens.

Given the anxieties and deprivations that children presently experience, and the challenges that face them in the future, they need above all else a deep sense of the meaning and the sacredness of their lives and journeys. It should be inculcated at home, in the churches, and at school, and by society in general. This message should replace by will or *fiat* all the dehumanizing filth presently showered on them from the media and other sources. Thus may they come to know not as many previous generations have been taught, that value comes from being competitive and ahead of others; rather, that their part in building and restoring the Earth is as important as every other person's part, regardless their intellectual capacity or the nature of their work or profession, and that the whole is greater than the sum of its parts. Enabling these beliefs in children will of itself change their energy from negative to positive. Add to it the self-help modalities that mute the Stress Response, then we can truly begin to build the Earth.

Though not impossible, it will be no easy task. The scriptures tell us that from the moment of our separation from Source, our human journeys are beset with ideas, ideologies and inclinations, pursuit of which can drive us deeper into separation and which, in the extreme, drive the chariots of divisions and wars. Concentrating on these distractions and pushing for supremacy within and over them, we so often fail to see that we are but a part, a sutra, in the tapestry of the whole. Christ Jesus said, "In my Father's kingdom there are many mansions." But he and others who have invited us to see the big picture are often misunderstood, dismissed as cranks, punished or killed as was Jesus himself. Amongst the most recent of these visionaries was Monsignor Ivan Illich, who founded C.I.D.O.C. — *Centro Intercultural de Documentacion* — in Cuernavaca, Mexico. During the 1960s and 1970s he used his Center as a forum for scholars of the world to discuss major issues of the 20th Century. Amongst these was the idea fostered by religious and other philanthropies to make available higher educational opportunities to all young people in Latin America. Noble as the intention may have been, Illich and his colleagues felt that if this higher education failed to fulfill its promise of an economically better life, due to the scarcity of opportunities to apply it in many Latino societies, then it could be counter productive. Their fears were not without experiential precedent. The commonly held belief in post-World War II Europe and in North America that higher education would prove the panacea for all the ills of society proved to be a mirage. European governments made higher education available to their young citizens through tax-supported government grants. Many of those who availed themselves of these opportunities, even to the level of doctorate degrees, found themselves jobless because of the lack of employment opportunities. By the late 1960s these highly schooled, credentialed but jobless people rioted in Paris, France and were declared re-dundant (useless) in the United Kingdom. Relating to a spiri-tual dimension far richer than any degree, Illich and his col-leagues pushed for a de-emphasis on schooling, which they labeled de-schooling in favor of promoting values of self-worth and respect for others.

At the very center of their polemic was that human worth and dignity are God-given — an inherent part of every individual — and cannot be otherwise conferred. Post-World War II experience in Europe certainly lent truth to the ines-capable fact that schooling and accumulation of degrees is *no* substitute for this eternal truth. However, these and other ideas were greatly misunderstood and led to an involuntary closing of C.I.D.O.C.. Tragically so, for the greater part of what was being promoted there is precisely what the world is so in need of: a common belief that every human being, regardless of eco-nomic, social or educational status, is an expression of the One, Eternal, God. Further, that each individual is on her or his own journey to a deep abiding awareness of this truth for them-selves and for others. Only by enabling it, and starting with children, will we be able to say, "I am Thou, Thou art I, and We are One."

That the treasures of spirituality are presently on a path of convergence with science is cause for hope. Eventually at their encounter, they will give lie to the ideas of Descartes that have dominated Western thought for too long. Mind, body and soul are *not* as Cartesian philosophy had us believe, separate entities independent of each other, but in fact a trinity of ex-quisite interdependence. Since the energies and memories within this trinity interact with each other, in searching for the roots of the disassembly of the human race, we need look no further than the assembly of energies and memories that have served to disengage it from its source in God. This begins at conception, continues through fetal development, birth and early childhood. In this context, we must be aware that the journey is not only that of the individual but of the whole human race. But, there can be no becoming to building the Earth without its beginnings in individual souls.

Quite recently, Dr. Stanislaus Grof applied the concepts of holography to an understanding of how body, mind and soul interplay as a whole. In essence, Dr. Grof codified the memories of conception and perinatal experience into what he calls four Basic Perinatal Matrices (BPMs). Perinatal is defined as the time interval between conception and the twenty-eighth day of postnatal life. [11]

The first matrix (BPM-1), which can be called the amniotic universe, refers to our experience in the womb prior to the onset of delivery. This means that what happens to the mother in terms of her thoughts, feelings and behavior become memories within the soul of the yet unborn child.

The second matrix (BPM-2) refers to cosmic engulfment with no exit. It pertains to our experiences when uterine contractions begin but before the cervix opens to liberate us.

The third matrix (BPM-3) refers to death and rebirth struggles of our lives and reflects our experiences of moving through the birth canal.

The fourth matrix (BPM-4) is the death and rebirth theme that is related to our experiences when we leave the mother's body.

Dr. Grof claims that each BPM has its own specific biological, psychological and spiritual aspects and that they not only incorporate the archetypes of Jung but are the memories from which we react to the circumstances of our human journey. Though his theories are fascinating, and from my clinical experience I believe have validity, his greatest contribution has been in the quest for re-birthing those souls with profound and dysfunctional emotional and behavioral disorders through Holotropic Breathing. In this endeavor, he attempts, as did the great psychologist Abraham Maslow, to de-pathologize the human psyche and to look at the inner core of our being — the spiritual center, not only as the source of metaphysical darkness and illness, but as the source of health and as the wellspring of human creativity which is at the heart of how we can change the energies within which we live. These concepts coincide with those of Dr. Viktor Frankl, one of the great psychiatrists of all time and founder of *Logo Therapy*, who has spoken and written eloquently about the need to touch and heal the energy at the spiritual center, the flow of which is almost always interrupted in psychiatric disorders.

As Aidan, our protagonist, told us, Divine energy is always present deep within. But nowhere is it more susceptible to ignition than in the souls of children. Children see life in sharp contours and brilliant colors, vibrant gifts of creation that reflect the transformative energy within their souls. Starting with the lights and shadows of their beginnings they are, rarely, if ever *not* in touch with the contradictions of their lives. And, given the brilliant energy of their colors and contours, can describe and relate to them with piercing clarity. Thus, regardless the extent to which deprivation, neglect, abuse and abandonment have been the give and take of their lives, they retain an instinctual knowing of their place and rights and even their responsibilities within creation.

Parents are or should be for love and yes, even tough love, which is in fact nurturance and supportive guidance.

Society is for protection.

When these cocoons fail them, they are eloquent in expressing their despair but also their hope. So, for the next three chapters, I will let them speak for themselves. For, as the Psalmists of ancient scriptures were the chronicleers of the rhythms of life and purveyors of advice on how to live it, so are the world's children the psalmists of today. Through their words, feelings, behaviors and use-age they are *lamenting* their profound sense of disconnection from the source of creative love and, at the same time, they are *singing* of their hope for it to be present in their lives. Therefore, I ask my readers to *listen* to what they have to say, *hear it,* and let it seep into your soul, for they truly have insights into the dilemmas of the world and thus clues to many of the answers to them. However, if we choose to turn deaf ears then this and future generations can become part of an unending cycle of rootlessness, irresponsibility and violence.

Notes

[1] John 10:10
[2] John 14:6
[3] John 14:12
[4] Luke 22:42
[5] John 20:13-16
[6] Reported during the nightly ABC News, March 18, 1996.
[7] Mark 14:36
[8] Bede Griffiths, OSB, *The River Of Compassion*. (Amity House, Inc.: New York, 1987).
[9] His Holiness, Pope John Paul II, *Crossing the Threshold of Hope*. (Knopf: New York, 1994).
[10] Nelson Mandela, *Long Walk To Freedom*. (Little Brown: New York, 1994).
[11] Stanislaus Grof, *The Holotropic Mind*. (HarperCollins: San Francisco, 1993).

VII

Life In Children's Own Words:
Through Betrayal To Hope

We look for the right, but it is not there;
for salvation, and it is far from us.
We look for the light and lo, darkness;
for brightness, but we walk in gloom.

Isaiah 5

For everything that lives
is Holy.

William Blake

In the beginning was the Word,
and the Word was with God, and the Word was
God.
He was in the beginning with God.
All things came to be through him,
and without him nothing came to be.
What came to be through him was life,
and this life was the light of the world;
the light shines in the darkness,
and the darkness has not overcome it.

John 1:1-5.

EVA

"*I wish I was never born.*"

"Why is that," I asked.

"*Because the beginning was so terrible.*"

"Oh, what happened in the beginning?"

"*Well, my mom was raped.*"

"How do you know that?" I asked.

"*Well, I feel it,*" she replied.

"Where do you feel it?"

"*All over, just all over.*"

"Did your mom tell you that she was raped?"

"*Well, she never talks about it. But I feel it. I feel dirty and I feel hurt all over. I wish I could begin again.*"

"If you could begin again, how would you like that to happen?"

"*I would like a lot of love around beginning again.*"

"Do you think it is possible for you to begin again even though you are now twelve years old?"

With a sly, shy look she said, "*How could that ever happen? I'm too big, I can't be born again.*"

Then I asked, "Are you sure you can't be born again?"

And again, with that shy look that had the quality of hope in it, she asked, *"What do you think?*

I replied, "Yes, I think you can be born again."

"Why do you think that?"

"Because I know that the source of all creation is right within you. And all that needs to happen is for you to be in touch with it.

"Well, how can that happen?"

"Why don't we, just for a moment, both of us, you and I, look out the window. And after looking out the window for a few moments, I want you to tell me what you see."

"Well, I see trees, I see sky, I see a little bit of sun - even though there is a little bit of snow on the ground. I see people walking on the road, I see cars going by, I see the dogs play-ing."

"Yes, and what do you think makes the trees grow?"

"Umm, I guess, sun?"

"Yes, but, a lot of things don't grow like trees just because the sun is there. The sun is there for everybody. So what else do you think the trees need?"

"Water."

"Yes. So we have sun and water. What else?"

"Well, I suppose it get food from the soil."

"That's right. It gets food from the soil. So, the soil nurtures it, doesn't it. And somehow or another, the sun and the water help that nurturance in a way that enables the tree to grow. But what do you think that makes all of these things to work together to make this beautiful tree?"

"Well I don't know."

"Well, do you suppose it could be energy? You've heard about energy, haven't you? Well, do you think energy is necessary for the tree just as energy is necessary for you?

"Yea."

"Do you suppose the energy that makes the trees grow and the energy that enables you to do all the things that you do share the same source?"

"Well what do you mean?"

Do you suppose that there is a Creator who makes all of these things come together so that each part of creation has it's own energy so that it can grow and multiply?"

"Yea."

"Well, if that's the case, then we share energy with all of creation, don't we."

"Oh, I suppose."

"Well, if we do, then we need never feel lonely."

"How is that?"

"If we share energy with other things, then we know that we are a part of this wonderful creation. So, no matter what happens in our own families, or how we came to be born, we know that we have something very special, something called creative energy, within us that allows us to be our own special and irreplaceable selves."

"Can you help me touch that energy because I would like to feel clean and whole."

"Yes, we can do that."

"Could we do it now?"

"Of course."

With deep breathing I then facilitated her own ability to go into deep relaxation and began the process of taking her gently back to her origin in Eternal energy. In just three sessions with my guidance she had changed the negative memories and energy she had felt all her life, deriving from the violence of her conception into feelings of being connected to God. The change was quite obvious. Her facial expression changed from that of anxiety to one of equanimity and her cheeks took on a healthy pink; the result of increased blood flow due to the effects of her present sense of connection releasing the Autonomic Nervous System into more normal functioning. Eva was in fact reborn and did well.

GABRIEL

I had seen Gabriel on many occasions. He was a very injured child; deeply anxious, profoundly depressed and all but closed down emotionally. His father had used him for child pornography. His mother, being overwhelmed by the situation - and herself being in fear of her husband who was physically, verbally and emotionally abusive to her, did what she thought was the best thing for her child and had him removed from the home by a court order. For this action, Gabriel harbored deep resentment towards her. It was fortunate for Gabriel that he was placed in a good foster home with wise and kind foster parents. I had counseled this child before he was placed in foster care at which time I had always found him to be extremely guarded and very withdrawn. Following the love and nurturing he received from his foster parents, Gabriel was able to open up considerably. At one point, after a few months with them, he gave the appearance of a young man who had suffered greatly, had come through a dark tunnel, and now conveyed self-assurance and a sense of his own identity. On this occasion, he looked me directly in the eye and his previous sad and hopeless look was not there. Rather, there was a serious and benign look on his face and he was able to talk to me in a more direct manner than ever before.

"Hello, Gabriel, how are you?"

"O.K."

"Just O.K.?"

"Well, yea, but that means I'm better. I feel good."

"Why is that?"

"Well, last week I spoke with my mom."

"That is marvelous. Tell me about it."

"Well, I told her how mad I was at her for not protecting me."

"What did she say?"

"She cried."

I then asked Gabriel to close his eyes and take a few deep breaths. When I saw that he was relaxed, I said:
"Now, Gabriel, just scan your body with your mind until you come to the place where you can feel what you were feeling when you spoke to your mother and she cried."

After a minute or so, he pointed to his heart.

"What does it feel like there," I asked.

"Good and bad!"

"Tell me more."

"Well, they're good feelings because I had to tell my mother how angry I was at her - it was a rage inside of me. But they're bad because of the reasons I had to do this."

"What did your mom say?"

"She said she was sorry and that she loved me."

"Can you give what she said a color?"

"Pink!"

"Fine. Now scan your body again and this time point to the place where you feel the bad feelings about what happened to you."

He pointed to the region of his Solar Plexus.

"What does it feel like there?"

"MAD! EMPTY!"

"Does it have a color?"

"Black."

"Would you like to change those mad black feelings?"

"Of course."

"Well, may we start?"

"Yes."

We did start, and continued for several sessions. It was significant that Gabriel pointed to his Solar Plexus when conveying his feelings about being abused by his father. The Solar Plexus is a relay station for the Autonomic Nervous System whose central role in maintaining balance of body, mind and soul has already been described. Being a pawn in his father's hands he essentially had no control over his own life and therefore, felt powerless. His thoughts and feelings of powerlessness, and the stress response they evoked, caused dysfunction of his Autonomic Nervous System – the effects of which he felt powerfully in one of its major relay stations.

Gabriel gave me much cause for joy. Through our counseling and healing sessions, which were directed towards changing the quality of his emotional and soul energy, he was enabled to be in touch with the dynamics of his situation.

Through his coming to understand the fear within which his mother lived, Gabriel became her healer. He saw that what appeared to be her lack of love and protection was actually great love and that having him removed from the home was the only avenue of protection available to her for him. His transformation reflected a not uncommon happening when these troubled children are enabled to be in touch with their own souls, they become the loving and healing parent to the injured child within their parents.

Gabriel's story is, unfortunately, not uncommon. During the 1980s and 1990s I saw many children who had almost identical experiences, some items of which are included in his odyssey.

DIANA

"Tell me, why do you think you were sent to see me?"

"Because I think everyone might be better off if I was dead - because everyone fights over me. I don't seem to be able to please anybody. My stepmother is a dope addict. My mother is in the hospital. And my father, well he just doesn't care."

"Well, on a scale of zero to ten, how much do you love your mother?"

"Oh, eleven."

"How much do you love your dad?"

"Well, I love him ten, and not eleven, because he doesn't hug me. He drinks a lot. He has tried to quit drinking, and it made me mad when he fell-off the wagon. My brother is three years older than me. He has abused me since I was six years old, so he only gets a five. He makes me feel YUK! Sometimes he says he's sorry, and then we're friends for a while."

"And then what happens?"

"Well, it starts all over again. He just uses the good times to get me to do what he wants again."

"And what about your mother's boyfriend?"

"I hate him. He beats me all the time. It makes me feel so hopeless"

"When you feel hopeless, what do you do?"

"I drink alcohol to feel a little happy for a little time."

"What does 'happy' feel like?"

"Don't know."

"Tell me more."

"Well, I don't feel 'it' anymore."

"Tell me about - 'IT'."

"You know, not feeling hopeless."

"Well, if I could give you your three dearest wishes, what would you ask for?"

"First, to have my real mom and dad to be together, and for them to be nice and good and for us to have a normal family, and for us to forget all this 'step' stuff - stepbrother, stepsister, stepmother, stepfather. It's ridiculous. Second, to be rich, because I'm poor and I'd like to buy expensive clothes. Third, perhaps I want to live forever because, although I think everybody would be better off without me, death kind of scares me."

"Do you think any of this could happen?"

"No."

"Why not?"

"I told you - it's hopeless."

I then went through the process of relaxation and changing the energy of the memories within her soul, much as I had done with Eva. Being more depressed and anxious, it took longer but when we parted her depression and anxiety had improved considerably. Despite all that had happened to this child and her feelings of hopelessness, the yearning within her soul for love, self-respect and to be respected by others remained very much alive.

Diana's story is but an example of many other children who experience trespass of body, mind and soul and yet retain a burning desire for *love* and a *felt connectedness* to their creative source.

RUTH

"Hello, Ruth."

"Hi."

"I hear that you have been having some problems. Would you like to tell me about them?"

"Well, I guess I am talking to you today because I have run away from home. My mom went to court and told them she couldn't control me."

(A period of thought)

"You know, my mom didn't want me. I think she was doing at my age what she thinks I'm doing now. She was running away and having affairs with fellows, and somehow or another I came along - out of one of her get-togethers."

(Some more thought)

"I haven't lived with mom all of my life. I was being sent out from my moms home because of her problems. And now that I am home, mom is very, very cruel to me. She hits me with anything she can grab: shoes, lamps and many other things. One time she went to school, grabbed me and pushed me down the steps to her car, yelling at me and telling me what a terrible girl I was."

"I told you, didn't I, that mom went to court and had me put away. But I ran away. And then, the police caught me. And that's why I'm here. What are you going to do for me? Did you know that my mom used to use drugs a lot. She may have been using drugs when she was pregnant with me. But she's better now. She's been clean for the last six years."

"Why do you think your mom brought you to court?"

"Because she knew that I was doing the same things that she was doing when she was my age, and even younger. And you know, I've had sexually transmitted diseases since I was ten years old."

"Well, what would you think would be the best way out of your very bad home situation?"

"Well, I'd like to be a singer and a model, and to live with my little sister and my stepfather. That way, because my mother and my stepfather are now divorced, I needn't be with my mother. And my little sister and myself can live with my stepfather."

"Is that all that you would like?"

"Yea, don't you think that's enough?"

"Do you suppose there could be something else?"

"Oh, yes, I'd like to have a lot of love in my life. But I'm not sure I know exactly what love is, except that somehow I feel that it wouldn't hurt anymore."

"What wouldn't hurt anymore?"

"Inside, of course, I wouldn't hurt inside."

"On a scale of zero to ten, tell me how much you love your family."

"I love my mother three, because she hits me, hollers at me, she did drugs. Although I have to say that she was much nicer to me when she was on the drugs because she wouldn't bother me. When she's not on drugs she nags me. Now, my little sister, I love her ten plus, and I love my stepfather ten plus. And if I could have a husband like my stepfather, then maybe in the future I would like to be a wife to a nice man and have children of my own."

When I asked her why she would like this, given her history

of a violent family situation, she replied,

"It's important to be married to someone you love."

"Why is being married to someone you love important?"

Looking at me as though she wasn't believing what she was hearing, she replied,

"Well, don't you know that love is the only way out."

"Out of what?"

"All this mess; boyfriends who don't give a damn and only want a part of you that satisfies them."

"Oh, tell me more."

"You know,..." (long pause)... "don't you?"

"Maybe, but you tell me."

"Well, if you are really married and love someone, they love all of you and won't hurt any part of you."

"Tell me about the part that hurts most when they don't love you."

Pointing to her heart, she said,

"Right here."

So, you told me that having children of your own is important. Why is that?"

"Well, I'd never let happen to them what happened to me. I'd love them."

"Is there any way you can think of that would make love and a happy family possible for you?"

"Yeah."

"What is it."

"Make boys believe that girls are people too."

"Anything else?"

"Yeah. Make me and all the girls feel that we don't have to do things that make us feel yucky."

"Do you think that's possible?"

"Yeah."

"Would you like to try just for yourself?"

"Of course."

As with so many other injured children, we embarked on a program of enabling Ruth to feel in touch with her beginnings in Eternal Love and Energy. Being so much in touch with the origins of her despair, she did well. Ruth's problems and anguish dramatically reflect the trans-generational nature of soul as well as experiential memory. Not wanted from the outset, she thus arrived in her mother's world as an encumbrance. Yet, when Ruth started to act out in a manner which was almost identical to that of her mother at a similar age, the rage her mother felt at what had happened to her violently exploded on Ruth whom, in her anguish and despair at her own life, she now perceived as the cause of her problems and her entrapment. Projection of the consequences of one's own behavior on others is a common manifestation of soul injury – thus, a frequently quoted psychiatric symptom. In this case, it's origins are readily perceivable and, in fact, the violent behavior of the mother reflected the yearning in her soul for love that was so eloquently expressed by her daughter.

MORAG

"You know, don't you, why I'm here to see you."

"I know what I have been told, but I'd like you to tell me."

"Well, life at home is very difficult. My mother's boy-friend is always nagging me. I can't stand it. I hit him a few weeks ago and he hit me back."

"What did you do then?"

"I called my father, he lives in New Mexico. He called the police at mom's home and when they arrived they took me to the hospital and I was in the psychiatric unit for two weeks. It's not fair. My mother's boyfriend should have been taken away, not me."

"How well do you know your father?"

"Well, he left my mom before I was born."

"Have you ever lived with him?"

"No. But we are very close."

"How is that?"

"Well, he understands me, he calls me from time to time and he listens to what I say. Besides, I don't like what my mom and grandma say about him."

"Tell me about that."

"They say he's no good, a dead-beat. One time it made

me so angry I ran away and they sent the police after me."

"Has he ever sent you birthday and Christmas cards?"

(Long pause)

"Sometimes."

"Do you have any brothers and sisters?"

"Yeah, I have an older sister who is three years older than me. My mom says that my sister's father and she were in love but he died soon after she was born. My mom and my older sister get along better because they are comfortable with each other. But mom is different with me. She acts like she resents me."

"Why do you think that is?"

"Well, my mom and dad were always fighting when she was pregnant with me. My dad hated her and he left her before I was born."

"So on a scale of zero to ten, how much do you love your mom?

"Only two, but I wish it could be more because deep down I love her."

"And your dad?"

"I love him 10."

"Even though you don't really know him?"

"Yeah."

"If I could give you your three dearest wishes, what would they be?"

"First, I would wish for my dad's back to heal and for him not to have anymore pain. Then I'd wish to be able to give my mom money to pay-off all her bills. I would also

wish to live with my dad."

"Do you think any of these wishes are possible?"

"Maybe not."

"So, then, what do you think about the future?"

"I like to think of what God may have waiting for me."

"What do you think that might be?"

"Well, I know I must be kind but I sure hope God will help me avoid bad situations like all those that I have known. My life has been so mixed up, but deep down I know that I am one of God's children; I go to Church and I try to help myself sort out all of my problems."

"Morag, you are a very sweet and loving and lovable girl - is there anything else you would like?"

"Yeah. To be married, have a good husband and lots of good and lovely children who will always be happy."

"Anything more?"

"Yes, I want to write poetry like Shakespeare and Emily Dickinson."

"Why is that?"

"Well, they knew about life, and so do I."

Morag was a very sweet and sensitive child. She was reacting to the confusion of events in her life and primarily from not being wanted from the outset, and the subsequent absence of love which she felt deeply in her soul. Her acting out behavior reflected *RADIEC. Yet, her song of hope for the future sang loud and clearly through and above all which in her life's experience she had to lament.

She is a shining example of the tenacity of the desire for love and connectedness to our creative source no matter how hopeless life has so far been. It is precisely this tenacity and desire that needs nurturance in every child's life. Morag was a joy to work with and eventually reached a point where she knew she had choices and learned to exercise them in a positive way.

*RADIEC-*Reactive Attachment Disorder of Infancy and Early Childhood (see note #4 pg.34)*

LAURA

Laura and I met when she was eleven years old. She was referred to me because of the intolerable situation she was said to be creating within the home. Her mother and biological father had never been married, but her mother had recently married her live-in partner of the previous seven years with whom she had a five year old son. Laura had greatly resented her mother's partner living in the home and, once her stepbrother was born, indulged in repeated beatings of him as well as hitting her mother and her mother's partner. She had had several psychiatric admissions to hospital before I saw her, all prompted by her violent behavior, none of which did anything for her. When I interviewed her mother, she told me that Laura was an unexpected pregnancy. She was only sixteen at the time, and felt very afraid and sad. When Laura was born she felt overwhelmed and realized, at the time I was speaking to her, that she had not given her the love and attention she needed, not because she didn't want to but because she was simply emotionally incapable of doing so.

From the outset Laura had not been wanted and, following her birth, her mother was emotionally unable to welcome her or give her the love and care she required. We know that if children are not held close to their mothers, skin to skin, within the first six hours of birth, that the chemistry in their brain changes in a way that leads to increased aggressivity; Laura was an example of this happening. These children always show signs of RADIEC, and Laura was no exception.

She was a bright and intelligent girl, and was well able to manipulate her home situation to the point of completely disrupting the lives of her mother, her boyfriend (later husband), and her half-brother. She was also very concerned with her own sense of what was right and wrong in other people's behavior, and disinclined to listen to other people's stories or even give any credence to the fact that they also might be having problems. Thus, due to absence of early bonding, she was not only deprived of a good beginning which continued to have a fall-out in her life and life's experience as well as on those around her, but she had also become turned in on herself and very narcissistic which would make it very difficult for her to make and retain meaningful relationships with either sex in the future. She would, I believe without the type of therapy that would change her energy, always be very self-centered, bouncing along the surfaces of life without any real involve-

ment with other people. She was, at age eleven, already showing pronounced symptoms of narcissistic and borderline personality disorders. She had little sense of personal responsibility and assumed none for her behavior - and perceived all of
her problems to be someone else's fault.

This absorption with self precludes feelings for other
people so, therefore, one's own inclinations and desires become
center stage. These are the people who go on to be able to
hurt, maim and injure other people and justify such actions as
being necessary on the grounds that in some way these people
got in their way! In a sense, it is the ultimate loss of self identity - one's actions being dictated by self-indulgence without
any reference to other people's feelings or needs -- a replica of
Aidan our protagonist. Her story is told rather than her words
because it vividly portrays the consequences of unwanted pregnancies which are followed by non-nurturance in the womb, at
birth and during infancy and early childood. The fallout is not
just on the child, it is on the family and all of society.

Actually, Laura was very adept at deep breating and
relaxation. Over time she was able to feel the rhythm and quality of energy in different parts of her body, and to give these
feelings colors. By grounding these good feelings through touch,
in this case using a small pink stone, she felt a deep sense of
acheivement when in potentially explosive situations by feel-

ing this stone in her pocket she was able to engage the good feelings generated during therapy. In fact, she was able to change her own neurochemistry.

JUDE

This child was ten years old when I encountered him. He had been through the court system because of repeated truancy from school. When I first met him, he told me how terribly sad he felt because his biological parents were separated and because they didn't love him. His father and mother were young when he was born and separated soon thereafter. Since that time, he had been bounced around from one family member to the next right up until the time I saw him. His mother, obviously, was a very injured person herself, had had many partners, and was presently involved with a younger man and expecting his child. Jude's father had been physically and emotionally abusive toward him on the ocassions he saw him before he was taken in by some relatives to whom he had become attached.

When I asked him why he was having trouble in school he replied that he felt angry all the time. And he added,

"When I feel angry, I loose it - I can't control myself. I want to punch everything and everybody in sight."
He had, indeed, been put on probation following physical assaults on other children in the school that he attended.

He said that he hated his father because he beat on him and because he treated his mom and his stepmother as badly as he treated him. He said that he wished his mom could be all right so that he could go back and live with her because he loved her dearly.

When I asked him how much he loved various family members, on a scale of zero to ten, he gave his mother 10, his dad one, and his half-brother nine. For the family that had taken him in and with whom he seemed to get along, he gave each one of them 10. When I asked him what his three dearest wishes were he replied,

> *"To have no record of bad behavior, ever.*
> *To live with the people who don't beat on me forever.*
> *To live happily ever after."*

When we talked about feelings, he told me that his feelings were sad and bad. He was sad when he thought that perhaps he might never again be able to live with the family to whom he had become attached. And he felt bad, because he knew that he had earned his own way into the court system and yet he felt that he could do nothing to control his emotions and his behavior. He expressed negative feelings toward teachers in school.

Jude was profoundly depressed and highly anxious. He was deeply in need of compassion. He possessed insight and honesty that were admirable. He had known uncertainty all his life, yet he retained a deep love and longing to be with his mother. He was confused as to why she had abandoned him - as she also had been abandoned as a young child. During our counseling sessions he was able to transpose his feelings of confusion to those experienced by his mother; thereby coming to have compassion for the dilemma she faced when at age 16, confused and afraid, she was left alone with him and didn't know how to cope. Eventually he moved into a deep desire to re-establish a relationship with her.

So often, when parents fail to be nurturing and loving, it is *not* because they are indifferent or intrinsically bad; rather, because they too are hurt people - it is trans-generational memory manifesting as aberrant parental behavior. Thus, I believe it is essential in counseling children to lead them into a felt compassion for the parent(s) that hurt them. Remaining angry at them obviously colors the quality of their own lives and contributes to continuing the cycle of dysfunctional feelings and behavior through unrelieved trans-generational negative memory.

VIII

*Life In Children's Own Words:
Their Hope & Despair*

Nature is never spent;
There lives the dearest freshness
deep down in things;
And though the last lights off
the black West went,
Oh morning, at the brown brink
Eastward, spring
Because the Holy Ghost over
the West world
Broods with warm breast
and with Ah!
Bright wings.

Gerard Manley Hopkins

Can a mother forget her infant,
be without tenderness
for the child of her womb?
Even should she forget,
I will never forget you.

Isaiah 49:15

Even before the term "nosology" was given to the description and classification of disease and dysfunction, clinicians diagnosed them on the bases of their signs and symptoms which had been observed over time. Nosology is, in fact, the codification of how the memories of encounter between humans and factors in their environment produce recognizable changes in form and function which are replicated within fairly narrow parameters each time any of these factors collides with a human.

Let us take Measles as an example. Each time a child or an adult meets with the Measles virus, depending on the degree of immunity of the individual to the disease it causes, some or all of the following signs and symptoms will occur: fever, cough, coryza, conjunctivitis, an erythematous, maculo papular rash, an enanthem, i.e., red mottling of the hard and soft palates and the distinctive Koplik spots which are white dots on the buccal mucosa. Complications such as otitis media, bronchopneumonia, croup and diarrhea occur more commonly in young children and encephalitis, which occurs in approximately one of every 1000 cases, can frequently result in permanent brain damage.

If there is complete immunity no symptoms will appear. With decreasing immunity the symptoms will appear with increasing severity. This, of course, is a lesson and a message from what takes place in physical immunity to what should be taking place in promoting immunity for the soul, a topic which I address in another book, *Immunology of the Soul*. At this juncture, however, what needs to be emphasized is the commonality of reaction of the human body to same or similar external stimuli, and how this is modified by actively or passively acquired immunity which, of course, includes genetic memories.

Classification and codification of psychiatric disorders has more or less followed the pattern set by physical disease. However, since psychiatric disorders are in fact disorders of the soul, what is codified in the DSM-IV is the commonality of response of the soul to the assaults that can bring it down and which are expressed as emotional and behavioral disorders and their accompanying changes in brain and body chemistry and function. Yet, when it comes to diagnosing psychiatric disorders in children, the criteria itemized in DSM-IV don't always fit nor do they remain static. By this I mean they frequently move from one diagnostic category to another. The reason for this is that the neural pathways of children are still developing and interlocking, creating the connections that ultimately influence behavior. They are, therefore, subject to constant change, changes that derive from their experience and the feelings and memories thus implanted in their souls. Of such is the *e-motion*, the energy in motion, within which they react to life and it's living, both subsequently and in the present.

An infant or very young child who is soul injured will show signs of withdrawal and failure to thrive. As it matures, and if this injury remains an unhealed wound in it's soul, it will from about the age of 2 - 8 exhibit signs of RADIEC, which are often diagnosed as adjustment and behavioral disorders which of course in the larger context of the child's life, they are. As the child grows into young adulthood, the consequences of injury to its soul will more closely resemble those of adult psychiatric disorders. In my experience, as a child moves into adolescence and then early adulthood, it is not uncommon to see them flow from one diagnostic category to another. Always the trajectory is from a diagnostic category where connection to reality is more or less intact, mostly the affective and personality disorders, to one wherein retreat from reality becomes its predominant symptomatology, the so-called dissociative disorders.

What is happening, of course, is the loss of self identity; a movement beginning with a separation of the self from the abuse that disallows self to be self, culminating in separation and disassociation from all that is external to it.

Several of the children whose stories follow showed this progression of symptoms which was more or less complete by the time they were referred to me. All of them showed signs either of Manic Depressive Bi-Polar Disorder, which I believe has as its roots the rage and sadness at the absence of nurturing parents or of borderline and other personality disorders. Most often there is a blurring of diagnostic categories, their behaviors being of mixed symptomatology. Thus do they render us insights into how psychic energy flows and is subject to change, a fact not always taken into consideration in the treatment and management of childhood emotional and behavioral disorders or indeed also those of adults. Too often we make a diagnosis that gets set in concrete and from which the child/adult is pigeon-holed for the remainder of their lives. All too frequently we treat these injuries to the soul with drugs. Drugs will never heal a soul injury; they will simply mute its expression. The gifts given to us by all the children whose stories are told, and the countless others whom they represent -- but particularly by Aliza, Micah and their companions in *Chapter VIII,* is the sure knowledge that even in the face of established psychiatric disorder the *energy* within the human soul is fluid and ever receptive to change -- surely a cause for joy and one to which we should give our loving and united effort to bring about it's promise of healing and wholeness.

ALIZA

Aliza was a very sweet 14 year old girl when I first met her. Her mother was the same age, 14, when she gave birth to Aliza. On account of her alcohol and drug abuse, she was unable to care for her. Aliza was placed in a foster home at the age of two and subsequently rotated through four foster homes in all before she was returned to her mother's custody at age 12. By this time her mother appeared to be in a stable marital relationship. However, due to Aliza's bouts of uncontrollable rage, which were often followed by periods of equally uncontrollable sobbing, plus her constant fighting in school, she was again placed in foster care at which point I was asked to see her.

She lost no time in telling me all about her problems. When I asked her what she thought might be the reason, she responded:

"Nobody likes me."

"How do you know that?"

"Well, people look at me the wrong way."

"Tell me about the wrong way."

"They look at me like I'm dirt!"

"So, what happens then?"

"I ask them why they're looking at me like that and if they give me a smart answer, I punch them."

"Then what happens?"

"They punch me back and we get into a fight."

"Then what happens?"

"It's always me who gets in trouble; but nobody realizes it. People are against me."

"How is that?"

"Well, no one loves me and it hurts inside."

"What does that feel like?"

"Like someone is pressing on my chest, trying to stop me from breathing. I can't breathe. It makes me panicky and I punch out."

"Can you give me a color for when this happens?"

"Black!"

"Where is the black when you feel mad?"

"All over. It goes from the top of my head to my toes, my ears tingle, my face becomes red, my teeth become clenched and I feel mad all over."

"Does the black and mad feeling go away?"

"Yeah."

"Then what happens?"

"I feel sad."

"Where do you feel that?"

"Same place, all over."

"Does it have a color?"

"Yeah, just gray."

"You know everyone of us sometime or another has wished for our lives to be different. If you had three wishes, what would they be?"

"My wishes would be to go home to my mother, to never be in trouble again, and to be happy."

"What does happy mean?"

"Don't know." (Pause) *"Do you know?"*

"Maybe, but you tell me."

"Just to let go of all these mad and sad feelings."
(Pause) *"Can you help do that?"*

"I think so."

And so we started our journey towards her healing. In the process, she came to know that because her mother had been deprived, as she also had been, of a nurturing family, she was unable to cope with the demands Aliza as an infant and toddler had placed on her - a situation exacerbated by her drug and alcohol abuse, which in itself was a cry for her own nurturing. Gradually Aliza was able to redirect the anger she felt towards her mother into an energy that allowed her to encounter her mother in a more understanding and loving manner.

Within this child, as with so many others, the acting out is an expression of their *laments* at their life's experience; their *song* is what remains at the center of their being and soul, the longing to be reconnected with love, with the source of their life, and with positive energy. Aliza expressed this longing very simply and eloquently in her three wishes.

She was one amongst hundreds of children who have given me *hope* for the future of humankind. For despite the odds stacked against her, she yet yearned for the opportunity to feel love in her soul and give it in abundance to others - especially to the mother who, on account of her own hurt, had not been able to nurture her with a mother's love.

LESLIE

Leslie's mother and father were separated soon after he was born and subsequently divorced. His mother then entered into a very abusive relationship with another man who, along with his friends, also abused Leslie physically and sexually. Leslie was removed from the home and placed in foster care. Subsequently, his biological father remarried and took him into his home. However, his step-mother did not like him and this caused great anxiety for Leslie.

His behavior became very aggressive, he showed signs of Attention Deficit Disorder (ADD) which no doubt were reflective of his deep anxieties and there were issues relating to the sexual abuse that he had endured from his mother's live-in boyfriend. Counseling was started and he was also placed on medication, but this was discontinued because it did not seem to help. He was then referred to me.

Leslie had known only horror in home and family situations. His profound anxiety and depression were expressed by his attention problems and aggressive behavior at school as well as at home. When asked how much he loved his dad, on a scale of zero - 10 he said, 10, his step-mother, six,

"because she yells at me all the time."

"What about your real mom, Leslie? How much do

~ 154 ~

you love her?

"I'm not sure, but I wish she could be well and I wish I could be with her."

"If I could give you your three dearest wishes, what would they be?

"To have dad feel well.
To find my real mom.
To live with mom and have a happy home."

"So, if you want a happy home, what would that feel like?

"Don't know."

"What would happy feel like?"

"Maybe like a Christmas green and a Christmas red."

"Tell me more."

"Well, Christmas is happy for a while."

"And then what does it feel like when it isn't Christmas?

"Don't know.

(Long pause)

You know, when I get mad I see a color that gets blood

~ 155 ~

red."

"When does this happen?"

"When I think of my step mom and my real mom's *boyfriend.*"

Leslie's agony at absent parents was quite obviously expressing itself in the alternating moods of rage and sadness, typical of Bi-Polar Disorder, and he was yet only eleven years old when I first saw him. Yet, the yearning for his mother and a happy home came through loud and clear. Both of his parents came from broken homes and very dysfunctional families. My counseling with him focused on how his parents really didn't know how to be parents, thus allowing him to defuse his rage at their denying him what was his rightful heritage. He was a very thoughtful child and did well; alas, all too soon his father and stepmother moved 100 miles away and he was sadly lost to my care.

TINA

Tina was thirteen years old when I first met her. Her parents were unable to provide for her or to parent her. Her mother had been hospitalized for psychiatric disorders and Tina had actually been in foster care for several years. Removal from her foster home became necessary when the foster parents divorced. The power of trans-generational memory in human behavior was very evident in this child's family. Even more amazing was the strength, the vibrancy of her desire to be connected with her source.

"Tina, why do you think you have been sent to see me today?"

"I have problems with being up and down all the time. I can be happy one minute, sad the next and then angry all over. I can punch pillows and then I hurt my dolls."

"How do you hurt the dolls?"

"I beat them."

"Where do you beat them?"

"All over, but Always in their hearts."

"Do they have hearts?"

"Not really, but I do."

"Do your dolls have feelings?"

"No, but I do."

"Tell me about your feelings."

"I can't feel feelings. It's like they're all locked up within my heart and sit above my head."

"Tell me about the feelings above your head."

"It's really weird. I have feelings that I can't feel. It's like they're floating in the air."

"Do you think you could connect yourself with these feelings that float in the air?"

"Don't know. It's like I have never felt like I'm fully on Earth."

"Why do you think that?"

"Well, I don't think that my mom wanted me."

"How do you know that?"

"I feel it."

"Did your mom ever tell you that?"

"Not really."

"Tell me more."

"Well, my foster mom tells me I'm crazy like my real mom."

"So, after that, what did you do?"

"I never talked to my foster mom about my real mom ever again."

"How did that feel?"

"Sad because I couldn't talk to anyone about my real mom and she's my real mom, you know?

"Could you talk to me?"

"Yeah."

"Of all the things you most would like to happen in your life, what would it be?"

"For my real mom and I to be together and for her to be well and for us to love each other."

"Do you think that is possible."

"No!"

"Why, No?"

"Well, my mom is crazy and she's in a hospital. They'll never let her out."

"Why is that?"

"When you're crazy, you're crazy. And if I can get a little bit crazier maybe I can join her and then we'll be together."

Thus did Tina in her own words describe the rage and sadness at the absence of parenting that is at the core of Manic Depressive, Bi-Polar Disorder. Also in her own words she described her anguish at being an unwanted child – *"I feel like I'm not on Earth."* Thus, she clearly showed the not infrequent flow of psychiatric disorders resulting from injury to the soul from one category, as described in the DSM-IV, to another. The first time I saw her, Tina already showed signs of flowing from Bi-Polar Disorder into frank Schizophrenia which was the reason her mother had been hospitalized.

The march of the memories of soul injury from generation to generation was in her case already well rooted. But Tina's gifts of imagination made her an ideal candidate for visualization and imagery during which sessions she was finally able to encounter her own feelings, give them colors and ground them. There are several ways of grounding, most of which involve the neural pathways of *touch*. The way she chose was by touching a bracelet on her wrist. Though she did well while under my care, nevertheless, because she had *no* close family ties on whom she could depend, relapse and eventual institutional care remained as a high possibility in her future – surely a cause for sadness and a call for us to do better for these children.

MICAH

When I first saw Micah, he was fourteen years old. He had been referred to me by the court for evaluation after his parents brought him there and told the judge they could no longer control him. They stated that he refused to obey their reasonable requests, was disruptive in the home, used obscene language and harassed them, as well as the teachers at school often violently. His parents, while well-meaning, were very inconsistent and ineffectual in their parenting of Micah. At one time they would be praising him for his behavior while ten minutes later they would condemn him for it, causing him tremendous confusion which was now erupting in rage. They had not set boundaries for him and were very withholding of their affection. Both parents had come from broken homes and had themselves been subjected to inconsistent parenting, a pattern they were now following with their own children.

Micah obviously had lots of soul injury since his troubles started very early in his life. He had been in counseling since he was six years old, and hospitalized on several occasions because of uncontrollable and often violent behavior. He had received numerous medications, none of which had helped. At age thirteen, he scored an IQ of 140 on the Weschler Intelligence Test which placed him in the 99th percentile of the I.Q.

range, and yet, of course, was failing in school due to his inability to focus his talents. When I saw him initially, he had all the symptoms of Bi-Polar Disorder. Bi-Polar Disorder, or as previously called, Manic Depressive Disorder, is I believe the souls reaction to the absence of loving parenting. It actually is the grief that devolves from rarely if ever being able to connect with one's parents. The predominant symptoms of this grief are alternating moods of rage, sadness and even despair – all of which he displayed in the extreme.

Soon after I saw him he began to indulge in more frankly dissociative behavior and became very contradictory in his statements. For example, he would tell me that he had threatened people in the past, but now would not do so unless they provoked him. At one session he declared,

"People are always on my back telling me I do bad things. But don't you think I have the right to have done something bad before I'm charged with it? I am so angry it makes me happy. There is a turkey on my shoulders telling me to do things."

Obviously, his soul's injury was moving from Bi-Polar Disorder into a frame within which he was dissociating from reality and becoming schizophrenic.

The tragedy of these young, intelligent and often highly manipulative people whose souls have been injured, due to their sense of isolation, is that, until they become independent, they are dependent on their parents. And, the only alternative, apart from allowing them to live with the parents and continue to disrupt the entire household, is to institutionalize them in some way. In Micah's case this was done, but it accomplished very little. He needed to turn around that profound, endless energy that he had which was expressing itself in anger. He needed re-birthing in order to redirect his powerful energy into creative pursuits. Given his intelligence, theoretically that would have been simple to do but, in actual fact the more intelligent the child sometimes the more they resist any kind of therapy, most often because they have a genius for negative logic that asserts they are fine and everyone else is sick.

Unfortunately, I lost contact with Micah when after a violent incident, he was placed in a high security institution. His story is told rather than his words because it is prototypic of thousands of others. Being the third generation in his family to be the victim of inadequate parenting, his story conveys the trans-generational nature of this and other so-called psychiatric disorders which are, in fact, unrelieved imprisonment of the soul.

ASA

Asa, aged 15, was the second of five children born to his parents. Both of his parents and their families had extensive histories of alcohol and drug abuse. His mother had her first child when she was fourteen and had experienced chronic depression since she was sixteen years old. When I first saw Asa he was fifteen years old and had already been in contact with the legal system. He was on probation on account of his fighting in school and having injured another child. He had also set fires. His parents described him as having two distinct personalities; one, very good and the other, defiant and aggressive. At their wits end, they were at the point of rejecting him completely. He had been referred for psychiatric help on many occasions due to his aggressive behavior and episodes of depression, none of which had helped.

Asa was one of the saddest looking children I had ever seen and was quite obviously suffering from profound depression. In fact, on the depression scales he scored in the range of severe depression and on the anxiety scale in the range of severe anxiety. At first he was very non-communicative, but eventually told me he was having problems at home and at school. I asked him,

"Tell me, what does that mean?"

"Well, I was fighting at school with all the kids and I yelled at the teacher."

"Why did you do that?"

"I don't know! But everybody bugs me at school."

"What about at home?"

"Oh, I fight with my brothers and sisters."

"Why?"

"I don't know."

"Does it bother you that you fight like this all the time?"

(Long Pause)

"Don't know."

In spite of his problems at home, when I asked him to tell me his three dearest wishes he replied with a very sad *"don't care"* look. Don't know, don't care. Coaxing him he replied,

"To go home. Have a new car that can go anywhere. Get older."

"Why would you want a new car?"

"Well - I could get away."

"From what?"

"Home."

"But you said your first wish was to go home."

"Well, not really - only - if they (the family) *change."*

"And what about being older?"

"When I'm 18 I can leave!"

"To go in the car and get away from home?"

"Yeah!"

Although Asa was, in general, non-communicative and appeared on the surface to have little insight, nevertheless, having a car and getting older was a cry to leave the home situation to which he also felt connected - if it could change. He wanted out of the prison of *home* but also wanted *in* it.

"Asa, what are your feelings about all of this?"

"I don't have feelings."

"Just close your eyes and take a deep breath. Now, imagine you have a heat detector in your right hand and, starting at the top of your head, scan it over your body until you reach your toes and tell me the places where you feel no heat, as well as the places where there is a lot of heat."

"It feels hot and cold." He had stopped over the place of his heart.

"Tell me more."

"Well, it feels happy but also like I want to cry."

"Why is that?"

"Don't know."

"Do those feelings have colors?"

"Yeah, like a rainbow."

"Which are the best colors in that rainbow?"

"Green and then dark red."

He was, of course, expressing his yearning for renewal (the green) and his anger at life (the dark red). As he continued his scanning, he said,
"It's all over."

"What's all over?"

"Black."

"What does black feel like?"

"I'm mad."

"Why are you mad?"

"Don't know. But it feels and looks like how when I'm mad I get into a rage."

"How does rage feel?"

"MAD!"

"Would you like to say good-bye to being mad?"

"Yeah!"

"Which color of the rainbow would you like most to have inside?"

"Yellow."

"Why do you choose yellow?"

"Because it is most like the sun."

"And what does the sun make you feel like?"

"Kind'a warm all over."

This child is yet another example of the sadness and rage at the absence of parenting and the feeling of disconnectedness this brings about. Although most children who have been the victims of dysfunctional or inadequate parenting from their conception onwards almost always show signs and symptoms of Reactive Attachment Disorder of Infancy and Early

Childhood, this child, in addition, had the burden of a very depressed mother following his birth who was unable to care for him. Obviously, the bonding that should have occurred between her and Asa did not occur and, instead, negative overtones were passed on to him. The pervasiveness of this experience, and the absence of positive bonding, was literally expressed in his body language and facial expressions - both of which were very negative and depressed and conveyed a sense of excessive sadness and anxiety. The sadness and anxiety combined, of course, would account for his ungovernable behavior. He was certainly at an age where he was flowing into frank Manic-Depressive Disorder.

Once the bond of trust had been established between Asa and myself he yielded to the desire deep within his soul to be freed from the prison of his despair. Given his deep depression and anxiety nevertheless, he had miraculously been able to express this desire in his three dearest wishes the first time we met.

He did surprisingly well with relaxation exercises. Also, he did well with visualization wherein with my guidance, he took himself to a place of peace which was a garden full of yellow flowers. Over time, and giving him the means to ground these peaceful warm feelings, he was able to engage and give expression to his many poetic and musical talents. As his confidence grew he chose not to live at home saying,

"If I stay well I can maybe help them to be well, but I can't do that if I'm there and have to fight them every day."

At age 18, Asa went to Junior College. Only the future will reveal what he does with all of his released positive and creative energy. But for now, I am happy he got a chance to climb out of his despair into a world of self-expression that could not only eventually break the cycle of despair into which he was born, but also hopefully bring healing to the family and home he obviously cared about and loved.

DARLENE

"Darlene, I think that you are very pretty."

"Oh, I don't think so - but, maybe just a little. Today I did my hair up nice - 'cause I was comin' to see you."

"Well thank you. But you know, apart from your hair-do, which is lovely, you are also very pretty. Believe that because I am telling you the truth. But, now, tell me what you think is the reason for your coming to see me."

"I fight with my stepfather. He beats my mom, he beats her up until she falls and he yells at me for nothing. I'm scared of him. He's mean. He looks mean and acts mean. My real dad is in jail. I don't know what to do except beat my stepfather for all he does to mom and me. I think it would be better if I died."

"Why is that?"

"Well, what else can I do to get away from it all?"

"We will talk about that a little later but first, tell me about your real dad."

"He's crazy. He's in jail. He left me and my mom when I was just a baby."

"Do you remember him?"

"No."

"Would you like to know him?"

"No, why should I? He's a jerk. He promises things and then doesn't do them."

"Has he ever given you something that you have kept - like a birthday or Christmas present?"

"Yeah. He gave me a doll once."

"What's her name?"

"She's dead."

"How did that happen?"

"Well, when I heard he was in jail again, I was so mad I ripped off her head."

"Did the dolly ever hurt you?"

"No, but he did."

"So, then, why did you hurt dolly?"

"Don't know, but I loved her."

"So, Darlene, now that dolly is dead, if I could give you your three dearest wishes, what would they be?"

"First, I'd want to go home - just to be with my mom. And I'd want my stepfather to be gone forever - in jail or dead, just like dolly.
I would want to never feel mad again, so that I won't have to go to hospital again.
And, last, to have a happy life."

"Tell me about being happy. What would that mean?"

I just don't want any more bad things to happen and I never want my mom and me to fight again."

"When you think about happy, what are the feelings like?"

"Well, I don't know. Maybe, nice."

"Can you give them a color?"

"Yellow."

"And what about the feelings when you are mad?"

"Well, it's like it isn't me."

"And do they have a color?"

"Black."

Darlene was a pretty and highly intelligent nine-year-old who had threatened to commit suicide. Her biological father had been diagnosed even before her birth as schizophrenic. He and her mother were divorced and her mother has subsequently married another man who is violently abusive.

The abuse she had endured and witnessed caused her to feel so hopeless that she wished to die. Yet, her desire to be connected in a loving way with her mother and with her own life comes across not only as her *song*, but as the primal cry for connection to all that would enable her to become truly who she was and is, a child of God; thus, liberating her from all the horror that stood in the way of this path. Already at the tender age of nine, her profound mood swings of rage and sadness were the all-to-obvious forerunners of bi-polar, manic depressive disorder. Darlene did well with relaxation exercises and she was able to create positive energy through imagry and visualization. She found peace and joy at letting these positive energies flow around her body because it gave her a good feeling inside.

IX

The Dying Of Children Is Their Own Experience

There is a spirit in the Soul,
untouched by time and flesh,
flowing from the Spirit,
remaining in the Spirit,
itself wholly spiritual.
In this principle is God,
ever verdant, ever flowing,
and all the joy and glory
of his actual Self.

Meister Eckhart

There is one common flow,
One common breathing;
All things are in sympathy.

Hippocrates

As adults, the memories of the instinctual knowings of our childhood becomes dimmed, particularly those that put us in touch with the cycles and rhythms of life and it's living, and death, and its becoming, in our dying. During childhood when the cycle of life is interrupted or abbreviated by disease or dysfunction, there is an ease of acceptance that becomes muted by longevity. As adults, we cling to life and not the rhythm, thus making of transition an event to be resisted. In our denial or even just our forgetfulness of the rhythm, we often and unconsciously, albeit with well-meaning, interfere with its flow in our dying children.

Teetering at the brink of the 20th Century, it seems to most, particularly those of us who live in the Western, technologically developed world, a rare tragedy when a child dies. And so it is. Yet, little more than 60 years ago, out of 1000 infants born in the U.S.A., between 80 and 100 died before their first birthday; and as many again succumbed before the age of five to the plagues of poliomyelitis, whooping cough, diphtheria, measles and other infectious diseases, as well as malnutrition. Today only seven of every 1000 infants born in the U.S.A. die before their first birthday, and only two between one and five years of age. Thus, only three generations ago, it was not uncommon for families to lose a young child - usually from acute, short-term and, because of their high prevalence, well understood and feared infections. If one puts this into the context of the extended family living three or more generations ago, there was hardly a family who had not fallen victim to the death of a child. This is no longer the case. Due to improvements in public health and the control of the killer infections of children due to universal immunization, the major causes of death in children are now predominantly chronic; long-term and not infrequently genetically determined diseases.

During the teen years, violence, sometimes self-inflicted, becomes the leading cause of death.

Thus, nowadays, in the technologically advanced world not only is death during childhood a relatively infrequent occurrence, but the causes of death cast different dimensions of burden and grief on parents, family and friends than those of a few generations ago. We also live in a success oriented society where death is not only vigorously denied but is widely considered to be the ultimate failure. All of this removes us as adults from being in touch with the rhythm and flow of living and dying, and adds considerably to the materialistic baggage and yen for money and possessions that we carry. So when dying and death touches a child we are shocked by its capriciousness and uncaring-ness and we are forced to re-focus on our own vulnerability and mortality. For parents, there is added a deep sense of failure and fear of what each or both may or may not have done to bring this about. This often involves pointing the finger of blame on the other which not infrequently leads to the break-up of the marriage and the family unit, thus having life-long fall-out on the parents, siblings and other family members. But for all who are or have been connected with the child, it also becomes a time of deep soul searching. Meanwhile, the child who is dying is almost always aware of these currents and finds a way of coping with them, either through withdrawal or consciously or unconsciously playing the part in the script presented to them at any given point in time.

In general, until they reach the age of nine or 10, the material baggage that children carry is minimal. Their focus tends to be on the energy and/or activity of the moment and, invariably, this carries emotional and soul overtones; *Am I loved or unloved? Secure or insecure? Am I doing the right thing? What do Mom, Dad or others think of me? How am I getting on?* Relatively unencumbered as they are with material baggage, they flow more freely with the ebb and flow of life than do adults, asking more for what nurtures their souls than what nurtures their bodies. Thus, in their dying, their nurturance resides in the loving touch of a parent, family member or friend; being surrounded by familiar toys and treasures of their own creation; for example, diaries, art work, and the like, to be able to feel and cuddle or pat a beloved pet and likewise, a favorite soft toy or doll, to hear a friends voice on the phone, or even the ticking of a clock.

Above all, and while they are still conscious, and no doubt even beyond waking consciousness, they yearn to be fully present to where they are at on their journey back to the source from whence they came. Thus do they give soul and meaning to the scriptural admonition, *"Remember man Thou art dust, and to dust you shall return."* And no one can say it more profoundly than the children themselves. Since this chapter in the *Psalms of Children* is filled with emotion, it needs to be brief. I have chosen only four children to tell of their dying. They do, however, speak for all of the children to my knowing and practice who had similar journeys to recount and for the multitude of children not personally known to me but who have traveled the same path back to their source.

ROBERT

I was walking through the out-patient department of the children's hospital one morning at about 6:00 a.m., on my way to see Megan, a ten year old who was dying of cancer. My journey was interrupted when I saw a young boy with a crutch struggling toward a bench which was situated between the emergency room and the out-patient department. Accompanied by his mother he finally made it, laid down his crutches and stretched out on the bench. He was very pale and struggling for breath and only had one leg. Though I had never seen this child before, being a clinician, I surmised that he was a victim of osteogenic sarcoma and had had his left leg amputated. His pallor and struggle for breath told me that his lungs were riddled with secondary deposits from his primary cancer; amputation of his leg having not achieved it's purpose. His mother, standing beside him in that motionless stance of unbearable grief, told me her child's name was Robert. I knelt beside this red-headed, pale, suffering and beautiful creation of God and asked,

"Robert, of all the things that you want most at this moment in your life that I could make possible for you, what would it be?"

His blue eyes looked into mine as if he were not sure of what he heard, but when I encouraged him and said,

"Tell me,"

he said,

"Tell my mom to take me home so that I can die in my own bed and with Rufie my dog beside me."

I turned to his mother and asked;

"Is it all right with you if I call his personal physician and tell him of Robert's wishes?"

In her catatonic grief she simply nodded,

"Yes."

Soon thereafter his physician arrived and, after hearing this wish for himself, allowed Robert to have his last wish. The next day Robert did die with Rufie by his side. Robert was ten years old.

MEGAN

The wisdom of children's knowing of the rhythm of life and death, and of the rhythm of womanhood, was told to me in a special way by Megan. She was nine years old and had endured the ravages of acute lymphatic leukemia diagnosed when she was only six years old. Hospitalized for another attempt of chemotherapy to arrest her dis-ease, her immune system had not only resisted this assault but was overwhelmed by it and thus closed down on its protection of her personhood. Nevertheless, she walked around the ward in her nightcap covering her bald head - a consequence of her chemotherapy, trailing her I.V. stand with its noxious elements behind her. Her aggrieved immune system was now completely shut-down and thus, no longer able to protect her. She thus was bleeding from all of the organs of her body. When the bleeding evolved from her vagina she was told she was having her first period. Cautious and protective of her last remaining ability to shut out all and everyone who was invasive of her personhood, nevertheless, since I was not her personal physician she allowed me to glimpse her soul.

"They say that I am now a woman. They are fools. I know why I am bleeding, I am dying and I am not yet a woman. Why don't they leave me alone?"

And so, for the next few days, when anyone came to her door she would pretend to be asleep so as to resist any further incursion on her suffering journey to the next dimension of her soul.

One day when I knocked on her door I saw one eye opening and the message was,

"Come in!"

"Megan," I said, "I am soon going to leave this hospital. Is there anything I can do for you before I leave.

Again, the message of memory came.

"YES! Tell my oncologist to stop all of this. Tell him to let me go home to be in my own bedroom and be with my stuffed toys."

Again, I became the messenger. This time, however, it involved some horrendous polemics with her oncologist who, unfortunately and emotionally, could not accept Megan's impending demise. Eventually she was allowed to go home. It was there that she died a week later. Megan was very aware of her impending death and of the games of denial being played by the adults in her life. Although well meant, the adults in fact impeded the peaceful flow of her soul into eternity. She in turn played the game of shutting them out and not wanting them around her, specifically not wanting to hear the un-truths concocted to *"protect"* her from knowing the truth of what was happening in her body, to which she herself and she alone was privy. Yet, her wish to be at home with all of her stuffed toys reflected her deep need for a loving human touch that would enable her to feel connected and safe in her dying; a touch denied to her because of the denying words to which she was subjected and which she didn't want to hear by those, including her family, who otherwise could have given her this comfort. Although her parents and grandparents grieved terribly, her legacy to them and to all of us, was a profound lesson in accepting where we are and then gracefully giving oneself to the rhythm and the flow of the journey.

MARK

One evening I was called to see Mark, a nineteen year old who had, by twentieth century standards, led a fairly tame life. Traveling in a car with other teenagers after a party, the driver lost control of the vehicle and hit a tree. Extracted by the "Jaws of Life", he was taken to hospital and found to be paralyzed from his neck down. Realizing the terrible future that lay ahead of him, he cried for death to take him. Yet, his sweetheart of three years urged him on to life.

"Do you have to walk to feel the wind in your face?" she asked. "Do you have to walk to touch the depths within your soul? Do you need legs to know and love God?"

Urged on by her faith and love, he took upon himself the mantle of hope. Then, disaster struck.

An embolus lodged in his lungs. In the second of several days it took him to die, he somehow managed to ask of me, his physician,

"Can I go home to hear the clock ticking?"

"What clock?" I asked.

"It belonged to my grandfather, and every night after my father died, I was only six years old then, before I went to

sleep I could hear it ticking. It connected me to my grandfa-
ther and my father whom I hardly knew."

He was, of course, speaking about memory; the memory of security and connectedness in his life. It is so strong in the human soul that even when we know that we are coming to the end of our earthly life, we long to be connected with the memories that have made us feel at one with life.

Hooked up to life support systems as he was, it was not possible to send Mark home. But we did arrange for the clock to be brought to the hospital and put near his bedside. With his sweetheart, Jane, and his mother by his side, Mark slipped peacefully into eternity. A thing as simple as a clock enabled him to feel connected to those he had loved and who had gone before him.

Thank you, Mark, for your life and your courage. Most of all, thank you for the message you left us if we have the ears to hear. Life means being connected to the source that brings us inner peace, security and love; and, sometimes, it is a small and material thing that makes this inner connection possible. And, thank you, Janie, for the love and hope you brought to your sweetheart in his living and in his dying.

CHARLOTTE

Many years ago when I was still a medical student, and when I had a Sunday afternoon off, I would visit a nearby Children's Hospital and Convalescent Home. Sunday afternoons were for visiting from family and friends, so I would seek out those children who had no visitors. Such a child was Charlotte. She was seriously ill with the cardiac effects of Rheumatic Fever. Week after week I visited her and each time her injured heart labored more and more furiously to sustain her to the point where her chest heaved with its every beat. But there was a deeper injury to her heart and soul. Neither of her parents ever came to visit her. This nine-year-old, unsung saint, child of God, explained,

"Mum and Dad don't get along; they fight all the time and blame me for their fights. Maybe they didn't want me."

Then one beautiful Sunday afternoon in an English springtime, so full of the promise of new life, and while I held her wax-like, skin-clad, bony hands, she asked,

"Will you stay with me until I die?"

I promised her I would and I did. At her funeral only her maternal grandmother, who was in a wheelchair, two of her nurses and I were present.

More than 40 years later, the suffering of this child remains deep within my heart and soul. All the more so, because when I was nine years old I contracted Rheumatic Fever. From an over-achieving, full of dance and music child, I became a slab of immovable protoplasm. For the next year-and-a-half with much love and prayer, my parents attentively nursed me back to health and eventually taught me how to walk again.

Since then there have been occasions when, under what seems at the time to have been unbearable grief and stress, the memories of the immovability Rheumatic Fever left in my body, mind and soul have returned to paralyze me physically. The reality of my inability to move and its metaphor for my soul becomes the prayer of acceptance of what I am enduring and have endured in my journey back to *one-ness* with the source from whence I came.

Thank you, Charlotte, beautiful child lying white upon your white pillow, for the grace and courage you gave to me to travel my path. Together we have touched many lives.

X

No Man Is An Island

God of my life, Incomprehensible, be my life.
God of my faith, who lead me into Your darkness –
God of my love, who turn Your darkness
into the sweet light of my life,
be now the God of my hope, so that you will one
day
be the God of my life,
the life of Eternal Love.

Karl Rahner

No man is an island entire of itself.
Every man is a piece of the continent,
a part of the main.
If a clod be washed away by the sea
Europe is the less as well
as if the home of thy friends or
thine own were.
Any one's death diminishes me
because I am involved in mankind.
Therefore never send to know
for whom the bell tolls, It tolls for thee.

Johne Donne

We must close our eyes
and invoke a new manner of seeing...,
a wakefulness that is the
birthright of us all,
though few put it to use.

Plotinus

The mystical vision of Karl Rahner and that of Johne Donne invite us, not to ethereal musings; rather, to the experiential realities that should be the underpinning and sustenance of our lives. At first glance we might be tempted to judge Rahner as being egocentric, searching for a very personal experience of God. But, to fully experience God is to experience all others who live and move and have their being in God as do we ourselves. John Donne calls us to this sense of "other" through his powerful imagery of the global interdependence of all humans, with each other and with all creation.

Put another way, their messages are those of Christ Jesus and the prophets of all religions who told us the *Way* to *Life* is to live with love for God and love for neighbor in one's heart and soul. But how can one love one's neighbor without first loving one's self? And how can self love self unless self is connected to God. Throughout the stories the children have told about themselves (except for the children who were dying) their sense of being disconnected from God is evident. None of them initially felt Go(o)d about themselves. Their life's experiences not only reinforced this negative energy within their souls but served to bring about a sense of separation from others with painful and sometimes crushing sequelae, not only for themselves but for all of society.

The following stories of Ivor and Randy convey more poignantly than any profusion of words, the horrendous and heart-breaking consequences of *not* fostering and nurturing in children a healthy God-centered love for themselves and respect for others. If we are to begin the work of healing humanity and building the earth we must, as Plotinus urged over 2000 years ago, *"invoke a new manner of seeing..., a wakefulness that is the birthright of us all, though few put it to use."*

IVOR

Ivor is now in jail. He is eighteen years old and he is in jail because he was involved in a murder. It was drug related. When I first saw him, he was very cocky and felt that he had the edge on life, and, thus, the edge over the lives of others inasmuch as he was making over one thousand dollars a week. At that time he was only thirteen. I lost track of him for many years and caught up with him after he had been sentenced to thirty-five years in jail with no parole. When I first saw him, in addition to him being cocky, he asserted that his greatest desire was to live forever and become a millionaire, and have everybody else be his servants. After he went to jail, this is what he said:

"It's an endless cycle. Someone influenced me to do what I did. I thought it was great. I influenced someone else, and they influenced someone else again. And do you know what? They get younger. I'm in jail now and the younger guys tell me I don't know what I'm talking about when I tell them to quit doing what they're doing, to go back to school and start leading decent lives.

'He's crazy man, don't listen to him,' they'd say.But now I'm in jail and I wanna die young. I just wanna die young. I want to die."

This young man was an unwanted pregnancy and was abandoned at birth. He lived with his grandmother who had two other grandchildren to look after. He grew up with as much love as she could give him. She had to work and, so, the children were looked-after by other people in the apartment building. By the time he was seven, he was on the streets looking for a living. By the time he was nine, he was a sophisticated drug dealer and managed to evade the law and keep from being murdered by other gang members until he was seventeen when he was caught in a drug-related gang killing for which he will spend what could have been the best years of his life in jail. As a child, he basically had nothing to give him an incentive to live. The memory operating in his life was one of abandonment from the time of conception, as well as a feeling that he was on his own. Did his experience of abandonment by his natural parents, and a hit and miss, mostly miss, nurturing experience from his overwhelmed grandmother, lead to his jailing? The answer is obvious.

RANDY

Randy was an engaging 13-year-old boy with the street smarts and savvy of a man twice his age. He had never known a stable family or home life and so sought out his own means of subsistence. Since he was eight years old, he had been a drug runner then a dealer in a major American city - and since the age of 10, he had been a user. The oldest of four boys born to a single mother, he had "seen it all." Miraculously, his life and how he processed it in his heart and soul had made him deeply wise in human and spiritual ways.

"I never knew my father and he never saw me. I know how hard it has been for my mom with four kids and none of the dads around."

"My greatest desire is to be a father to my three younger brothers because I don't want them to end up like me!"

"Maybe it's too late, I hope not."

"Like me," meant that at age 13, he was infected with the A.I.D.S. virus through use of infected needles while mainlining hard drugs. Randy expressed eloquently what I have

also heard from countless other children. Betrayed as they have been by life and it's experiences, the inner desire to be whole in oneself and for others to be likewise resonates with hope. Though he was painfully enduring his fate and was facing death, nevertheless in a deeply spiritual way he had become whole. Through counseling, not only was he beginning to love whom he really was, as a child of God — and so, fulfilling the first great commandment, but through his love and concern for his brothers he was fulfilling the second, "Love thy neighbor as they self."

XI

Change Is The Constant of Life: Ushering In the Promise of Life For Children

'For singing to our God is good.'
Rabbi Elimeleckh expounded thus:
'It is good if but man can bring about
that God sings with him.'

Tales of the Hasidim

Dive deep, O Mind,
into the ocean of Divine Beauty.
You will discover a new gem
instant after instant.

Sri Ramakrishna

For my thoughts are not your thoughts,
nor are your ways my ways, says the Lord.
As high as the heavens are above the earth,
so high are my ways above your ways
and my thoughts above your thoughts.

Isaiah 55

The currents of energy that flow from the souls of these children converge in a torrent towards common destinations. Above all, is their desire to be loving and spiritual beings and for this to begin at their beginnings. Thus, not only are they saying that every child should be conceived in love and lovingly nurtured within the womb but thereafter, that family should be the cradle of nurturance, protection, guidance and support. Further, by their fine attunement to the energies of the world, they are telling us that none of this can happen without fundamental changes in human values and attitudes. Most importantly, they are crying, if not yelling, for their voices to be heard and for the adult world to cease from treating the symptoms of their despair, in ways that serve only to perpetrate it, from generation to generation. The intent of their desires is incontestable. Indeed, the absence of all they wish for in terms of their own and family well-being is often at the center of religious debate and political rhetoric. Therefore, it could be tempting to put closure on this book, leaving the eloquence of their messages to reverberate in the Universe for all with soul to hear and translate into healing remedies. To do so, alas, would be a betrayal and a terrible disservice to them and most likely also to future generations.

First, because societies everywhere are beginning to speak openly about the present generation of children as having *no* conscience. At the same time society is attempting to instill conscience in a way honored only by time and mindless habit by committing offenders to correctional and prison facilities, graduates of which are notorious for repeating their crimes. Second, we live in a political and economically driven world where the voices of children, save those who commit heinous crimes or are the victims of crime, are seldom if ever heard. Rather, it is people who have made the cause of children their life's work who speak on their behalf, either personally or when representing agencies and organizations whose stated mission is the welfare of children. Third, when we match what children feel and say they need with needs and priorities set for them by agencies that speak on their behalf there is a basic difference of emphasis and few points at which they meet and match.

Putting all this into perspective requires that we focus again on the powers of memory and consciousness and the energies that drive them. Until and unless we factor them into our understanding of *how* they interplay to control the constant biochemical and energy conversations between body, mind and soul we will never be able to bring about the changes necessary for the true healing of the many faces of their disequilibrium.

Though these issues have already been addressed in some depth, nevertheless, they can bear further emphasis. Speaking for the great minds that share his awareness of the pivotal role of consciousness and its many energies in human behavior, His Holiness the Dalai Lama made the following observation at the Conference on Inner Science in California, 1985: "Western Science," he said, has displayed admirable determination in dealing with problems of Outer Science and has done so for the most part in a rigorous, rational and technically exacting manner." He expressed the hope that it would now apply the same discipline and devotion to Inner Science – that treasure chest yet to be explored that will enlighten and educate each individual to understand him or herself: to control negative emotions and distorted notions and enable him or her to journey into their particular highest potential of love and wisdom. "If we do this," he concluded, we will succeed in triumphing over the great danger of global holocaust." In his recent book *The Evolution of Consciousness,* Robert Ornstein addressed these issues by stating that "we need to teach both children and politicians how the mind (within us) really works; we need to explain to journalists how sensationalism affects and misleads the brain and we need to think of humanity as one interlocking organism, rather than a patchwork of nations tribes or individuals."[1] And in his latest book *A Brief History of Everything,* Ken Wilber not only proposes that the evolution of human consciousness is a spiritual journey but also renders his ideas in concepts that mirror some of those conveyed by one of the greatest thinkers of this century, Pierre Teilhard de Chardin.[2] Wilber traces this journey from its first cause and beginnings in matter, the cosmos, to the biosphere which is *life,* within which all matter and its many energies pulsate and interact with the *mind,* which is the consciousness that permeates all life and energy, even to subatomic and quantum levels and maybe beyond. Its ultimate or omega point is the noosphere, which may be defined as the end point of the journeyings of human consciousness and the beginnings of *all* being subsumed into *one* which is eternal, divine energy. The spiritual journey is the completion of the circle that brings *all* in *one* back to its origins and first cause. This journey has been, I believe, a continuum of creative love whose interruptions and blockages have been and continue to be the disconnections that permit energy to become negative. When this occurs, form and function lose their intended identity and become dissonant. I have referred to this phenomenon in greater depth in previous chapters, but by way of adding a further dimension to it one can relate it to the concept of *Morphic Resonance* as described by Rupert Sheldrake.[3] He maintains that in as much as all matter is made of fields of energy, which energies carry memories, then physical effects derive from the memories inherent in the fields of energy that organize matter. If the energy of these memories is blocked or interrupted then abnormalities of normal form and function will ensue. Transposing this to the memories and energies that drive thoughts and feelings wherein conscience dwells and which manifests as behavior - if it (conscience) is to be allowed to re-enter the world of children then the interruptions and blockages to the circle and cycle of creative love that have caused its dysfunction need to be removed and its energy restored to positive function. From the stories the children have told, it is quite clear that early memories reside within their souls. And, though they will often tell you passionately that they don't know why they behave as they do, what their behavior in fact reflects is the dissonance resulting from the interruptions that have occurred in their inherited energies, which could be interpreted as deviations from their intended morphic and functional resonance.

However, from what has already been said, it is obvious that once memories of negative response have been established it is that energy that drives the biochemistry of feeling and behavior. Likewise, once encoded in the genes, the negative response travels through time from generation to generation. Therefore, to simply suggest or even command someone so afflicted to stop and change is as useless in the long-term as expecting fundamental change to occur from time spent in programs currently offered in the correctional and prison systems, where for the most part therapies that can change the energies of destruction are not employed.

What is required is nothing less than a primal conversion, which means changing the memories of response and their biochemistry at or before conception.

Though lifestyles designed to prevent the onset of dysfunction and disease are becoming increasingly popular, nevertheless, we still have a mindset of the dominant norm in medical practice as being correction or amelioration of that which is already abnormal in form and/or function. Therefore, the suggestion of *primal conversion* may at first seem startling. However, recent advances in fetal surgery and the possibilities inherent in genetic engineering are expanding our awareness about the power of early intervention and prevention of long-term crippling effects. If possible for physical disabilities, then why not also for afflictions of the soul? Of all human suffering, that which has its fallout on many others, and often on society in general, through its presence in just one person are those behavioral and psychiatric disorders resulting from the soul suffering of disconnection from the source of creation and love (first cause) - that culminates in violence. It took only one Hitler to decimate an entire generation.

The power of the mothers thoughts on the developing nervous system and "mind" of her child is beyond question. In addition to the evidence I have already cited in previous chapters, recently published results of long-term monitoring of children born to women participating in the *Longitudinal Survey of Youth*, begun in the U.S.A. in 1979, showed that children of mis-timed or unwanted pregnancies exhibit more fearfulness, less receptive vocabulary and less positive interaction with their mothers.[4] In addition, they had lower scores for positive affects and self-esteem. By deduction this confirms that if a mother is existing within negative energy — such as depression, disillusion, conflict, etc. — at the time of conception and during pregnancy, this negative energy will be passed on to her fetus and continue on through the independent life of the child.[5] When one considers the almost uncountable number of children whose conception and intrauterine experience has been as just described, can there be any doubt of how the sum of this negative energy operates at many levels to bring violence into the world. In the September, 1996 issue of *Newsweek*, an article about the children of rape in Bosnia and Rwanda describe the extreme of this.[6] Many of the children of these rapes were abandoned at birth, and those who weren't will forever be despised and rejected because of the ethnic hatreds that begot them. Rape is the ultimate violence on the sanctity of creating life and, while the United Nations Tribunal in the Hague has ruled rape to be a war crime, no one expects the perpetrators to be brought to justice.

This article and the research quoted give a powerful voice to the pleas of children to be wanted and loved as Eva and others have told us, right from their beginnings. In order for this to happen, it reinforces the urgency to provide *parenting* education to young people which was one of the major recommendations of the researchers who conducted the study. Since 1965, when research led me to uncover the onset of the present epidemic of teen pregnancies, I have believed that young people need to be taught the many spiritual and emotional nuances of conception and pregnancy and of how the thoughts, feelings and energy, rather than just the sex that they bring to begetting a child can impact on the entire world.[7] Twelve years ago I wrote a research proposal to do just that, with targeted populations in different geographical areas and with well-defined measures of research outcome. Long-time researcher though I am, I was not prepared for the almost total lack of willingness to be involved in such a venture. Though there was a lot of interest in the proposal, it was not hard to pinpoint the reasons for the general unwillingness to be involved. The health care business is driven by reimbursement for services rendered for sickness, disease and ill health. A project such as the one I proposed would under this system of payment generate no revenues. However, within a generation it would not only drastically cut expenditures for symptoms and ill health consequent on negative energy, but would bring real health and well-being of body, mind and soul to individuals and families, thereby also to society. By so doing it would seriously cut back on services for which the so-called health care conglomerates are presently reimbursed.

The issue is achingly simple, but the path to its resolution not to be trodden by the faint of heart and purpose.

Must we continue to be held hostage by those who hold the purse strings of the status quo in the so-called health care and social welfare systems? Can we find a way to give real substance and legitimacy to the many voices of healing presently clamoring in their various but singularly focused way to say that treating the symptoms is *not* the way.

If *not* the way, then what is the way?

In fact, nothing less than a radical change in how we perceive health and its absence, all of which will engage our awareness of energy and the controlling power of its forbears - memory and consciousness.

The children have told us, and continue to tell us in fearsome ways, that negative energy, bad or hurtful memories, and the feelings of powerlessness and hopelessness within their consciousness are the reasons for their disconnectedness that expresses itself in angry and anti-social behavior. And when this is considered unacceptable, they are, more often than not, subjected to "hearings" in court whereupon the judicial system decides their fate. In spite of whatever degree of kindness lawyers and judges may treat them, just the very fact that they are there becomes another memory of abandonment and abuse, a deep scar on their souls that reinforces within their consciousness feelings of powerlessness and despair. Judgments and dispositions made on these children may be compared to judgments made by reading a few pages in the middle of a book, without reference to the whole story that has a beginning and an end. The beginnings for most of them have been full of the absence of respect for whom they are as children of God. Frequently, if not always, they are born to parents - in all socio-economic groups - who have been similarly afflicted. Thus, the energy within which they operate is transgenerational both in terms of genetic memories and the experiential memories of parenting.

The *end* of their stories will forever remain the same, until and unless the manner in which we address their healing and thus the healing of their children and future generations is changed. To give life and personhood to what I am saying let me tell you about Jeremiah. Born unwanted to a single mother who herself was the child of a single mother, she brought him to court when he was thirteen years old, declaring he was beyond her control. He had on several occasions been beaten by his mother's boy friend when he, Jeremiah, intervened to protect his mother from the beatings she was enduring from this man. Unable himself to endure the situation in this so-called *home*, and despairing of life in general, Jeremiah began to distance himself from it by staying out late and being truant from school. Following his court appearance which he told me, and I quote, was "the pits," he was placed on probation, one of the conditions of which was that he be at "home" every evening by 7:00 p.m. Unable to abide by this stricture, when he broke the terms of his probation he was hauled back to court and placed in detention. Scared to the depths of his knowing, and also scarred in his soul, he yelled to be let loose. The response was that he was manhandled to the floor and held there by the knee of a 200 pound detention officer placed in his lower back and with his arms pinned behind him in what is euphemistically referred to as a "butterfly hold."

When I saw him shortly thereafter, he was covered in bruises and scuff-marks that told of his agony of fear as he tried to loose himself from this stranglehold. And we call this "correction" for a child, wounded by the absence of love but with the power of it still in his soul that tried to protect his mother from the physical and emotional violence of another human who likewise had been injured by its absence. What he needed in those hours when he was alone and scared in a previously unknown and intimidating environment, was the presence of someone calm in demeanor who could assist him in defusing his fear by reassuring him in word and *touch,* and the energy of a loving presence that would call forth within his own being the relaxation response. What he endured from a system supposedly there to protect him was a continuation not only of the absence of love but also of the violence of touch.

Touch – it is a wonderful word with a myriad of universal meanings. It is the energy of touch that begets all life; and it is the quality of the energy of touch at our conception and birth that initiates the electro-chemical energy and, thus, the biochemistry that becomes the basis of our future emotional and behavioral responses to others and the world. As we journey through infancy and childhood the quality of the touch in our lives either enriches or diminishes our capacities to give and receive love, as well as to feel safe and secure or otherwise. When couples are married and ministers are ordained, the presiding clerics touch them on their heads as a symbol of the sacraments they have received. While touch can be a universal affirmation, it also can be a universal denigration. In fact, touch has a powerful modulating role in the biochemistry of our perceptions and reactions to all that is exterior to us and of how we perceive ourselves. Thus, it plays a central role in the development of personality and the behavior with which personality is so often identified. Touch is frequently that of which we speak when we express *E-Motion;* that is, energy in motion. We say, "I was touched..." by whatever happened. It is thus the language of our giving and receiving - the pathway to our soul. Its pervasiveness in our lives is unassailable, and of all our senses it is like the first language that we hear and then speak — the last to leave us before we die.

But something terrible has happened to TOUCH, particularly as it affects children.

In the sex crazed world in which we live, we have relegated touch to the sewer of pornography and suspicion. Teachers, child care professionals and other adults who work with children are afraid to touch them lest their touch be interpreted or construed as sexual molestation or assault. Notwithstanding the real presence of these evils, nevertheless on a far greater scale the re-creative and healing powers of touch are being lost to all children - particularly to those most in need of healing and affirmation.

No one who has seen Michaelangelo's "The Creation" in the Sistine Chapel in Rome can fail to be moved by the message and power of the *touch* between Creator and that which is created which conveys endless possibilities of life. Likewise, no one who has journeyed with children and adults alike who have been denied the touch of creative love can fail to be moved by the emotional and behavioral consequences of their disconnection which causes great suffering for them. When in my office, the most consistent response of these individuals so deprived is to reach for one or another of the many soft toys I keep there which without prompting they hug and stroke.

For over twenty years, Dr. Dolores Kreiger has preached, taught and practiced therapeutic touch. In her book *Accepting Your Power To Heal,* she describes in physiological terms what therapeutic touch can do.[8] The first response is a very rapid relaxation response, in many instances occurring in as little as 2-4 minutes, and isn't this what Jeremiah needed as indeed do all of his soul brothers and sisters and their parents. The relaxation response, which can be elicited in several ways – of which affirming touch is one — not only accelerates the healing process even in broken bones but has its most powerful effect on the Autonomic Nervous System (ANS) to which it brings the energy of rebalance. This is highly significant because dysfunctions of the ANS are at the heart of psycho-somatic illnesses which account for 75% and more of all illnesses. The soul of these illnesses lies within the anxieties and distress that derive from disconnection from the source of creative love. Yet, we live in societies that have chosen to spend their fortunes on the technology that supposedly repairs the damage done to the trinity of body, mind and soul by these disconnections as well as by the absence of human loving and healing touch. In the U.S.A., 70¢ of every health dollar is spent on administering this technology and drugs to people within the last six months of their lives, and then for a "benefit" of 10-14 days more of so-called life.

Is it any wonder then that there are debates and debacles taking place all over the world on how to pay for health services and contain their escalating costs, that in many western countries now consume 10% and more of their gross national products.

What has been lost is our focus on health. Re-fo-

cusing on health rather than its absence would within a generation, if not a decade, ease and possibly solve the financial crisis that too often is identified as the health care system itself.

Are we crazy?

Well, yes and no.

Yes, because knowing what we know if we have the will to *change* the system as it is, we could do so, and since our sense of connection to source begins at or before conception instituting *parenting* as a required part of the school curriculum for boys and girls should start immediately. And lest anyone thinks this is just a dream, implementation of parenting classes are scheduled to commence in September, 1997 in schools in Wales. The content of the parenting curriculum will address the psychological and emotional, as well as the physical aspects of parenting. And obviously, parenting should be a required component of pre-natal care. A similar but more broadly based program is one recently developed at the Worchester Polytechnic in Massachusetts. Designed for male college students and titled *The Passage,* its director calls it a holistic movement into adulthood. "Students are isolated today," he observed, "and they need the acknowledgment and wisdom of older people."[9] Worthy and commendable though this may be, such programs need also to be targeted to much younger age groups of both sexes.

No, because as presently structured, the Health Care System thrives on the use of expensive technology and drugs, and through these industries and the vast bureaucracies that have mushroomed and engulfed the Health Care System, it ends up supporting millions of people who are neither givers nor recipients of health services. These are vested interests that will require time and tact for conversion.

With these powerful behind-the-scenes controllers of the system, is it any wonder that when government revenues come to the vote for funding of various programs, those for children often get trampled by the rush to protect these other vested interests. Experimental programs funded by private and non-governmental agencies of which in the past there have been several fair equally poorly in the long haul. In 1988, Daniel and Lisbeth Schorr enthusiastically described 24 such programs in their book *Within Our Reach: Breaking the Cycle of Disadvantage*.[10] In 1996, more than half of them are gone. Commenting on this, Daniel Schorr says; "Foundations fund innovative programs for several years with the expectation that when they work public funds will pick up the cost; that is an illusion, it doesn't happen. Anything you want to do in a big way requires Government funding."[11]

With this as a backdrop, recent statistics beg questions as to how we can be so blind as to what is happening to the children of this nation and of the world. For example, a 1996 report by the US Department of Health and Human Services revealed that the percentage of children in extreme poverty, i.e., with family income less than half of the official poverty level, has doubled since 1975.[12] This doubling effect represents 10% of all children - which in hard numbers is 6.3 million to which must be added the ranks of the merely poor which include 1 in every 5 children. In 1992, there were 850,000 substantiated cases of child abuse, to say nothing of unsubstantiated and unreported cases. During this same period the homicide rate for teens more than doubled. Those who understand the trajectory of childhood development say these statistics project a grim future for American society.

Douglas Nelson, Executive Director of the Anne F. Casey Foundation says,

It may well be that the nation cannot survive as a decent place to live or a world class power or even as a democracy with such high rates of children growing into adulthood unprepared to parent, unprepared to be productively employed and without that sense of responsibility that leaves them unprepared to share in main-stream aspirations.[13]

With such dire predictions it appears hard to understand why legislators, for the most part, tend to overlook the special needs of children while at the same time are so vocal in castigating their socially unacceptable behaviors and lack of conscience. Could it be that they themselves are not adequately informed about the dire consequences of their lack of attention to what is *really* not only a national, but global emergency? More than likely, this is so.

A 1995 report on how state legislative leaders view children's issues and the people who ardently lobby for them discovered a vast chasm of mis-understanding and mis-communication between them.[14] Few of the 177 legislative leaders interviewed could even name the child advocacy organizations in their own State, and complained that those who act on behalf of children apparently do not fully understand the legislative cycle, often arriving too late in the budget cycle for any action to ensue. So, while there is a general belief supported by polls that most people are in favor of programs for children, somehow this resists translation at the legislative level. Obviously, just expecting legislators to do what advocates perceive as the right thing for children is not enough. They must be given arguments as to why it is in everyone's interest to do so. Furthermore, given the less than stellar results of the many generously funded programs in the past, all noble in intent — notably those authorized by the *War on Poverty*, plus the failure of the Welfare System to accomplish what it was intended to do, it is hardly surprising that legislators are wary of further involvement in what must appear to them as more of the same. In a sense, no one can fault them for that, but the fate of the National Commission on Children demonstrates the extent to which their aversion continues to operate despite the statistics that spell *crisis*.

Established in 1988 by the US Congress the mandate given to its 36 members was to develop policies for children's services in both the private and public sectors. This they accomplished by first of all defining six themes of need from which their final recommendations were made. These themes were:

1. Children in Poverty;
2. The crisis in health care;
3. The need for School Readiness;
4. The pervasiveness of drugs;
5. Reorienting services to children so as to enable and promote prevention; and,
6. The critical role of parents and other caring adults.

In presenting the Commission's report to the U.S. Congress that had established it, Senator John D. Rockefeller said,

> Many of today's children will reach adulthood unhealthy, illiterate, unemployed and lacking both moral direction and a vision of a secure future. This vision of the future is morally unacceptable and all of us should find it economically, politically and culturally unacceptable.[15]

What happened?
NOTHING!
As far as I could ascertain from my many inquiries, the report has been shelved.

Incongruous though it may seem for one who has been

an advocate for children for over three decades, to even think what next I'm going to say, nevertheless I believe that within all of this apparent unconcern for children and its many contradictions, there is a golden lining of immeasurable beauty and timeless usefulness. Its threads can be found both within what children express as their needs which are uniformly and fundamentally food for the soul, and their needs as perceived by the advocates who speak for them - whose emphasis, though by implication not devoid of soul, is clearly on physical (body) dimensions.

To give emphasis to what I am saying, in a special report entitled *What's Really Worth Doing For Children*, which was published in *Contemporary Pediatrics* in March, 1996, most of the recommendations both for the general population of children, as well as those considered at high risk were directed towards monitoring of physical health (Figure 11.1). Yet, all of the children whose stories are herein told, when asked what they most desired replied either directly or indirectly, that what they most needed in their lives was *love*. Frequently, as if to explain what they meant by love, they would make reference to their need to be free from feelings that caused them stress. In essence, what they ask for is the means to be connected to their spiritual heritage and to have the means of self-regulation. Could it be that within the apparent dichotomy between what children say they need and what their care-givers say they should have, that Universal Wisdom and energy is trying to get our attention? I believe the answer is, yes!

No one who browses in book stores or receives book catalogues in the mail can fail to notice the present plenitude of books that describe how health may be attained by bringing balance to the interplay of body, mind and soul. Coincidentally, people all over the world have in the last 20 years in

Figure 11.1

INTERVENTIONS RECOMMENDED FOR THE PERIODIC HEALTH EXAM:

BIRTH TO 10 YEARS

- Screening

> (Height and weight, blood pressure, vision screen [age 3-4 yr], hemoglobinopathy screen [birth], phenylalanine level [birth], T and/orTSH [birth])

- Counseling
    - Injury Prevention
    - Diet and Exercise
    - Sexual Behavior*
    - Substance Use
    - Dental Health
- Immunization
- Chemoprophylaxis

High Risk Population:

Population	Potential Interventions
Preterm or low birth weight	Hemoglobin/hematocrit
Infants of mothers at risk for HIV	HIV Testing
Low Income; Immigrants	Hemoglobin/hematocrit
TB contacts	PPD
Native American/Alaska Native	Hemoglobin/hematocrit; Hepatitis A vaccine; pneumo coccal vaccine
Travelers to developing countries	Hepatitis A vaccine
Residents of long-term care facilities	PPD; hepatitis A vaccine; influenza vaccine
Certain chronic medical conditions	PPD; pneumococcal vaccine; influenza vaccine
Increased lead exposure	Blood lead level
Inadequate water fluoridation	Daily fluoride supplement
High-risk sexual behavior*	Screen for gonorrhea, HIV, chlamydia; hepatitis A vaccine
Injection or street drug use*	HIV screen, hepatitis A vaccine
Blood transfusion between 1975-85*	HIV screen

* Intervention recommended for the public health exam for 11-24 year olds.
*Adapted from **American Pediatrics** (March, 1996)*

creasingly sought surcease from their ailments and have pursued health and well-being through alternatives to what is offered to them in the insurance financed health care system dominated by allopathic medicine. In the USA alone, it is estimated that out of pocket expenditures for alternative care amount to $14 billion a year. But what about children?

Quite obviously, and no doubt without having read few if any of these books, children are tuned into this same kind of energy of need for balance in their lives. The question then is how may we give them the tools of self-regulation that adults are scrambling for in record numbers? Very simply, by applying the principles of cyber-biology and cyber-physiology. These principles are in fact at the center of all the messages to be found in the present abundance of literature that treats of the connections and interdependence of body, mind and soul. The prefix "cyber" derives from the Greek, meaning that which steers, the helmsman; when translated to the Latin it means to govern. Attaching "cyber" to biology means governing our bodies and attaching cyber to physiology refers to the ability to control and govern our physiology. But why, one may ask, is this important? And what, if anything, is its relation to memory and consciousness and the energies that drive them which, throughout this text, I have emphasized as being so pivotal to whom we are and what we may become?

Very simply, *everything*!

The energies of memory and consciousness are as it were behind-the-scenes messengers to our thoughts and feelings which then prompt and monitor our behavior. In their turn thoughts, feelings and behavior have a reciprocal relationship with the Autonomic Nervous System (ANS) which, by virtue of its control over every non-voluntary function of our bodies, is the conductor of our physiology. Thus, the electro-chemical and energy conversations that take place between it and all systems of the body not only determine the quality and efficiency of their functions but bring to those functions the energies of memory and consciousness. The ANS is itself controlled by the hypothalamus, a small but mighty piece of gray matter situated in the mid-brain. After consulting with the Limbic System, which monitors our emotions and every other system of the body — including the Endocrine and Immune Systems — the hypothalamus then relays these filtered and conditioned messages of how to perform to the ANS. All of this is then processed through the cerebral cortex where our conscious thoughts reside. These interactive conversations never cease so there is always an accessible and active point of entry whereby their timbre can be altered which, nevertheless, demands a conscious input.

However, when for whatever reason and at whatever level there is a blockage to the free flow and interaction of these electro-chemical messages and energies, the normal physiological function cannot occur. The body will then go into *The Stress Response* which, if severe enough, will cause disease and dysfunction – the nature of which is determined by the weak link in our genetic and trans-generational memories, all of which has been described in Chapter IV. This being so, then learning how to mute the *Stress Response* and reverse its effects should be the obvious centerpiece of all health promotion and care. Furthermore, because skills that last a lifetime are more easily learned in childhood such instruction should be required courses in all school curricula.

Muting and reversing the Stress Response induces its opposite, *The Relaxation Response.* It requires only that we learn how to consciously inject ourselves into the constant internal electro-chemical chatter and conversations that at any point in time is our physiology. To do so is remarkably simple and, once a technique has been learned, it can be used over and again, anywhere and at any time. It requires *no* pills, *no* visits to the doctor, there are *no* side effects and the empowerment of knowing how to be self-governing lends confidence and serenity to our lives.

It is generally agreed that there are four prerequisites for bringing forth the Relaxation Response:

1. A quiet environment with a minimum of sensory distractions.

2. A mental device which can be a word or a phrase repeated silently or aloud, or fixed gazing at an object, to help the mind to move away from distracting thoughts.

3. A passive attitude, i.e., allowing intrusion on one's mental device to come and go as irrelevancies.

4. A comfortable position to minimize muscular tension.

With these four conditions as background, one then induces the Relaxation Response by following any one of many time honored ways whose shared entrance to the kingdom of relaxation resides within the breath, with deep breathing being the door. From earliest times and in all religions of East and West, prayer, contemplation and meditation have been and continue to be the path to balance of body, mind and soul and the reconnection of ourselves to one-ness in God. The use of a word or mantra while breathing deeply is currently a universally employed method.

Derivatives of Emil Coué's method of auto-suggestion, all basically forms of self-hypnosis, and the many techniques of systematic bodily relaxation pioneered a century ago by Dr.

J. H. Schultz — who named his method, *Autogenics* — are also widely used. The precise method is not important for each produces the same physiologic results namely, decreased respiration rate, heart rate and oxygen consumption; a lowering of blood pressure in those in whom it is elevated, and frequently a decrease in muscle tension. Likewise, brain activity is slowed and its electrical rhythm moves from the rapid beta (β) rhythm of involved activity to the slower alpha (α) rhythm of focus and calm. These physiologic changes are frequently accompanied by subjective feelings of inner calm, peace, love, forgiveness and even the ecstasy of a felt union with the Eternal Spirit of God.

Self-regulatory modalities are in essence vehicles whereby individuals transform cognitive or language coded information into a physical, physiological and/or emotional response. To be effective they must be made at a level at which there is processing capacity. Thus, evoking the Relaxation Response in children requires knowledge of their developmental capabilities. For most children 7 years or older, deep breathing accompanied by silent self-affirmation is often all that is required to kindle the positive energy resident in their souls. However, given their fertile imaginations, the techniques of Imagery and Visualization can be used from a very early age and for all ages. Using these as a basis, children in fact learn self-regulatory controls faster and more easily than do adults.

Countless studies report how children have been successfully trained to turn around undesirable habits, moderate anxiety, and the many symptoms associated with chronic diseases and pain. In addition, controlled studies have documented the abilities of children to self-regulate peripheral temperature, transcutaneous oxygen, brain stem auditory evoked potentials and many other physiological and patho-physiological processes. Most recently it has been shown they can self-regulate certain immune responses.[15] This and other research leaves no doubt that early training of children in self-regulation provides important preventive and therapeutic interventions for them, thus leading to an enhanced quality of life for them and for society. For children who are emotionally and behaviorally dysfunctional, it could prove to be their salvation.

All children have a great propensity to day-dream which means they naturally flow in and out of altered states of consciousness with great ease. A therapist knowledgeable about child development, and skilled in working with children, can make use of this ability and enable a child to go into deep relaxation with very few preliminaries. The voice quality of the therapist and a conveyed energy of loving acceptance of the child are important components in this dynamic. However, imprinting the energies and feelings of relaxation in their memories requires the engagement of their imaginations, and grounding them for future use requires relating them to *touch*.

Over the many years of my practice I have developed simple ways of accomplishing all of this. In our preliminary encounters, in addition to allowing them to tell the stories of their life's experiences in their own words, I ask them amongst other things to tell me about their favorite and least favorite colors, sights, sounds, people and places. I ask them to attach feelings to each of these items. Then, during therapy sessions, after assisting them to flow into deep relaxation, I invite them to a journey of their own threading and weaving — all the while asking them to show me the places in their bodies where they feel the feelings of all that they are experiencing throughout the journey. When they pinpoint good feelings I ask them to give a color and texture to them. Then, at the end of the session, from the cache of stones and snippets of cloth that I keep in my office I let them choose one of each. Then I ask the child to transfer the good feelings to the stone and cloth by rubbing them with their hands and sometimes also by placing them on the location in their bodies where they felt them — this is usually over the heart. Subsequently, they carry both in a pocket and are instructed to touch and rub them whenever they are faced with a situation that could make them feel sad or mad. The object, of course, is to enjoin the memory of good feelings that have been planted in the neural pathways of *touch*.

Most children need practice for this to become an instinctive reaction; therefore, practice time should be a part of their school day, especially for children with emotional and behavioral problems. Taping therapy sessions for future and daily use, while being an obvious way to enhance these skills, is not always a realistic option. The children most in need of therapy are initially too distracted and unfocused to independently follow through on using them. However, adding biofeedback to children developmentally able to use it and interpret it adds a further dimension of empowerment for them. Indeed, research has demonstrated that children take pride in being able to demonstrate, via biofeedback, their control over various physiologic responses. Their families are similarly benefited as are also their school peers and teachers when they learn the rewards of personal responsibility through the simple application and practice of self-regulatory techniques. From the age of eight, I believe combining relaxation methods with bio-feedback should be a weekly part of the school curriclum.

There are, of course, other ways of bringing about these physiological and subjective changes, some with an emphasis on changing energy from negative to positive overtones. Latterly, some of these modalities have been subsumed under the title "Re-Birthing," a reference to the biblical injunction that unless a person be born again of the Spirit he or she will not have life.[17] The energies within children are in a constant flux. Accessing them and then directively changing and grounding them usually presents little difficulty to those who have been trained to do this. Changing the quality of energy — re-birthing — is a powerful therapy for children who bear the burden of negative energies surrounding their conception, intrauterine and peri-natal experiences; likewise, for those who suffer from Reactive Attachment Disorder of Infancy and Early Childhood (RADIEC). Yet, because we live in a society expectant of quick fixes, dependence on drugs to "fix" children is sadly all too pervasive. Although there are instances where drugs may be indicated and even helpful, in the vast majority of cases they are *not* the answer. Indeed, giving drugs to children is a still-to-be-told tale of possibly terrible burdens on their immature and still developing nervous systems and neural pathways. Indeed, in the future we may learn that the use of psychotropic drugs may have added to their problems. In this regard we should learn from the consequences of the over-use of antibiotics which has resulted in their diminished effectiveness and the emergence of resistant strains of micro-organisms.

The many faces of scars of the soul are the expressions of memories of disconnection from our source — that *no* drug can permanently heal. From all that has been said, it would seem that only by changing the energy of the memories, and thus their expression in consciousness by using self-regulatory techniques can this ever be accomplished. Juxtaposing what it is possible to do for children in this regard which is for the most part not being done, particularly for those most in need of soul healing, in the mainstream of their otherwise usually well-covered physical management begs the question — *why*. Within this text some answers have been defined. However, in the ultimate, it begs a radical re-thinking of whom we are and how we come to be. This will require not only the *will* to change our out-worn concepts but the *imagination* to foresee the blessings of doing so.

Putting all of this into the broad picture of society in general, conveys a perspective of how urgent it is to begin *now* to give tools of self-regulation and the benefits of inner science to all children. Highlighting this urgency, Dr. Berry Brazelton, Professor of Pediatrics at Harvard Medical School and who was a member of the National Commission on Children, recently observed that "we are raising a generation of children in stress. All families are in crisis," he said, "not just poor families. Nuclear families with both parents at work, single parents, divorced parents and re-married parents are all raising children in stress."[18] Add to this the impact of their exposure to violence and one is left with no other conclusion but that children from all socio-economic groups are daily confronted with the fall-out from stress.

Confirmation of the appalling dimensions of stress in children resulting from violence was documented in an article published in the September, 1996 issue of *Pediatrics*, the journal of the American Academy of Pediatrics, which should gain the attention of all who are concerned with the impact of violence on children. Eighty-nine percent of pre-adolescent children from a suburban middle school and 96% of pre-adolescent children from an urban middle school reported knowing someone who had been robbed, beaten, stabbed, shot or murdered; 57% and 88% respectively actually witnessed a robbery, beating, stabbing or shooting and 40% and 67% respectively had been personally beaten, stabbed, robbed, shot or caught in gun cross-fire. Many students reported symptoms associated with somaticization syndromes, depression and post traumatic stress disorder. Both student groups in addition had witnessed episodes of victimization – mostly amongst family members or friends and expressed feelings of fear, anger, sadness and frustration about these episodes. Although most of the children spoke to someone about their exposure to violence, rarely was this person a health professional. Data such as this serves to give emphasis not only to the almost unbelievably high prevalence of violence and of its injurious and long-term sequelae to children, but also to the patently obvious non-relevance and non-penetrance of most current programs designed to combat it and to assist children in dealing with its many disabling legacies.

In speaking of Eternal mind, the prophet Isaiah declared:

My thoughts are not your thoughts,
nor my ways your ways.
As high as the heavens are above the earth,
so high are my ways above your ways
and my thoughts above your thoughts.

And, though the Psalmist declared: "Singing to our God is good," Rabbi Elimeleckh pungently added, "But – It is good if man can bring about that God sings with him."

Our physiology is the work of eternal mind and it, together with our souls and all our being, yearns to be connected to its source in God. Then, *all* that enables us to be thus connected should be lovingly developed, nurtured and protected. Thus are we enabled to walk through the dark places of our journeys for all life is a wave pattern whose valleys must be trodden and explored as well as its hills.

Stress is killing the minds and souls of children, and through the addictions they adopt to mute their pain so also is stress killing their bodies. The paths along which we have pursued surcease have failed. We are called to *change*, radical change: in how we conceptualize the origins, the nature and the management of this all-consuming stress. Nothing less than empowering children to self-regulate is urgently called for. Teaching them the principles of cyber-biology and cyber-physiology should become a national priority as should teaching health professionals how to teach them. Instructing parents and child health care providers should likewise become as much a part of routine child health supervision as administration of immunizations presently is and they should certainly be added to routine pre-natal care for expectant parents. Furthermore, with the present trend towards school-based health clinics, health professionals who staff them should be thoroughly trained and skilled in these modalities and should be allowed one school period for each class each week to teach them and fine tune them with all children. Unless and until we do this, we will continue to see an escalation in anti-social and violent behavior and addictions of all kinds. If we follow trajectories of the development of psychiatric, emotional and behavioral disorders as I have previously described them, by applying cyber-physiologic techniques at an early age, we can intervene to delay or prevent their manifestations. And need I add how important it is to encourage the daily and frequent practice of prayer from infancy on.

Humanity interacts with humanity from the many storied domains of memory and consciousness – and the belief systems of our adult lives – from which flow our feelings and behavior derive from the energies of their beginnings. Thus, if we are to moderate the trauma of world-wide violence, as well as allow the flow of the energy that connects us with our source in God and with one another, then we must begin to do so with children and their beginnings.

We must begin now.

Notes

[1] Robert Ornstein, *The Evolution of Consciousness*

[2] Ken Wilber, *A Brief History of Everything*. (Shamabala Publications, Inc.: Boston, MA, 1995).

[3] Rupert Sheldrake. *A New Science of Life* (Cambridge University Press, 1981); and, *The Presence of the Past* (Cambridge University Press, 1988).

[4] Longitudinal Survey of Youth, U.S. Public Health Service.

[5] Family Planning Perspectives (Nov/Dec 1995).

[6] Stacy Sullivan, "Children of Hate: Born Under a Bad Sign." *Newsweek* (September, 23, 1996).

[7] Ursula Anderson, "The Medical, Social, and Educational Implications Of the Increase in Out-Of-Wedlock Births." *American Journal of Public Health* 56, 11 (November, 1966).

[8] Dolores Kreiger, *Accepting Your Power To Heal: The Personal Practice of Therapeutic Touch*. (Santa Fe: Bear and Company Publishing, 1993).

[9] Ben Gose, "Worchester Polytecnic Program Helps Students Face Adulthood. *Chronicle of Higher Education* (Dec. 6, 1996): .

[10] Daniel and Lisbeth Schorr, *Within Our Reach: Breaking the Cycle of Disadvantage*.

[11] Margaret Blood, "The Children's Crusade," *Time* (June 3, 1996).

[12] US Department of Health and Human Services

[13] Margaret Blood, "The Children's Crusade."

[14] Ibid.

[15] Quoted in "National Commission on Children," *Pediatric News* (June, 1990).

[16] Wayne Rusin. "Relaxation Methods and Children With A Range of Illnesses," *Pediatric News* (November, 1988); see also, L. Kuttner, *American Journal of Clinical Hypnosis* 3, 30-34, 1988 and *Pediatric Annals,* March, 1991; and K. Olness and G. Gardner, *Hypnosis & Hypnotherapy With Children* (Grune & Stratton, 1988); Mark Smith, "Biofeedback, *Pediatric Annals* (March, 1991); William C. Wester, Donald J. O'Grady, *Clinical Hypnosis With Children* (Brunner Mazel: New York), 1991.

[17] John 3: 3-8.

[18] Berry Brazelton. *Pediatric News (June, 1990).*

Epilogue

*Let the children come to me and
do not prevent them;
for the Kingdom of God belongs
to such as these*

Luke 18:16

*Only a breath are mortal men
an illusion are men of rank,
In a balance they prove lighter
all together than a breath.*

Psalm 62

*Life is more than food
and the body more than clothing.*

Luke 12:23

*Resplendent and unfading is wisdom.
And she is readily pursued by
those who love her.
And found by those who seek her.*

Wisdom 6:12

The children have spoken, they have sung their songs and keened their laments. Science is speaking, and its forthcoming marriage with spirituality is promised by their recent engagement. We are teetering on the brink of new awarenesses of whom we are, how we came to be and what we must do to heal our brokenness.

The sufferings and yearnings of children invite us to a feast of discoveries about the role of energies in our lives, which in turn, invite us to discard our outworn and limited concepts of the genesis and management of dysfunction and violence. The marvels of technology have been based on harnessing an infinite variety of energies with promises of more to come. The time is now to harvest human energy – both transgenerational and experiential, to nourish and make new the human soul. It can be done and, when it is done, no more will the unwanted, neglected and abused sisters and brothers of Aidan, our protagonist, ever say again –

"My aching heart has turned to stone!"